D1621187

The Observers Series
MOTORCYCLES

About the Book

Clearly illustrated, with enough detailed technical data for comparisons, this practical reference book is useful for those who know about bikes and those who wish to learn about them. The world's manufacturers are listed alphabetically by name and country and a cross-section of their popular road-going models can be found arranged in engine size order. In trying to capture a genuinely international representation, from a market dominated by a few, very large Japanese manufacturers, it has been necessary to select from the extensive range of machines currently available.

This seventh edition concentrates on the 1990/91 models and describes, in most instances, motorcycles with UK or European specifications. Because two-wheel road-users share a unique experience and have much in common, the book includes some mopeds and scooters but the emphasis is on the full road-going motorcycle range of each company. Bikes which are not intended for street use are left out of this book, but readers will be able to find a selection of dual purpose trail or enduro machines which can be ridden on road and across country. A brief explanation on the technical specification, given for each model, will be found at the front of the book.

About the Author

Robert Croucher writes about motorcycles because he enjoys riding them, he is fascinated by the history of their development, he is intrigued by the ingenuity of design that goes into their manufacture and he admires the daring of those who race them. In short, he likes the world of biking! A riding experience that included many miles on Hondas, a Ducati and several BMWs has led him to the conviction that the roadcraft skills and understanding that come with regular biking are excellent foundations for all road-users.

He believes that this book will have served a purpose if it settles an argument between enthusiasts over model differences, if it conveys a clear picture of the variety of motorcycles available to the rider around the world today or it inspires the reader to look more closely at what biking can offer as an experience in a mobile, yet energy and safety-conscious society.

The *Observer's* series was launched in 1937 with the publication of *The Observer's Book of Birds*. Today, over fifty years later, paperback *Observers* continue to offer practical, useful information on a wide range of subjects, and with every book regularly revised by experts, the facts are right up-to-date. Students, amateur enthusiasts and professional organisations alike will find the latest *Observers* invaluable.

'Thick and glossy, briskly informative' – *The Guardian*

'If you are a serious spotter of any of the things the series deals with, the books must be indispensable' – *The Times Educational Supplement*

O B S E R V E R S

MOTORCYCLES

Robert Croucher

BLOOMSBURY BOOKS
LONDON

PENGUIN BOOKS

Published by the Penguin Group
Penguin Books Ltd, 27 Wrights Lane, London W8 5TZ, England
Penguin Books USA Inc., 375 Hudson Street, New York, New York 10014, USA
Penguin Books Australia Ltd, Ringwood, Victoria, Australia
Penguin Books Canada Ltd, 2801 John Street, Markham, Ontario, Canada L3R 1B4
Penguin Books (NZ) Ltd, 182–190 Wairau Road, Auckland 10, New Zealand

Penguin Books Ltd, Registered Offices: Harmondsworth, Middlesex, England

First published 1976
Seventh edition 1991

This edition published by Bloomsbury Books, an imprint of
Godfrey Cave Associates , 42 Bloomsbury Street, London, WC1B 3QJ,
under licence from Penguin Books Limited, 1992

1 3 5 7 9 10 8 6 4 2

Printed and bound in Great Britain by
BPCC Hazells Ltd
Member of BPCC Ltd

ISBN 1-8547-1053-2

Introduction to the **Seventh Edition**

As they enter the 1990s, motorcycle manufacturers are optimistic, even though sales world-wide remain depressed. The new decade has seen a welcome comeback for several well-known marques. The Harley-Davidson success story continues in the States, hopes are high for the relaunch of British names like Norton and Triumph, and two famous Italian companies, Benelli and Laverda, have made a return with exciting new models.

The unexpected political changes in Eastern Europe have meant that former Communist Bloc manufacturers such as CZ, MZ and Simson will now be subject to open market competition. Their cheap, simple models will not, in future, be competitive. While they are rushing to bring out modern, upmarket designs, companies such as BMW in a united Germany, Moto Guzzi in Hungary and the Japanese Four across Europe are moving in on new opportunities for expansion.

The high costs of buying, running, insuring and maintaining modern motorcycles, the persisting concerns for the safety of young, immature riders and the demands for ever-more stringent compulsory training, continue to deter people from biking. However, a new market has been identified: older enthusiasts reliving their youth and able to recognise the value of two-wheeled transport on congested roads. For the price of a very ordinary saloon, the 'born again' bikers can experience Porsche or Ferrari-type performance. One European survey has estimated that the use of motorcycles instead of cars by commuters would save them up to two weeks a year in their travel time to work. Other studies have shown that sales and service people can make up to twice as many calls a day in crowded city centres when they use bikes rather than cars.

Concept designing has resulted in a huge number of special models aimed at particular segments of the two-wheeler market. Tourers can choose from the full-dress Honda Goldwings, the Harleys and their big lookalikes from Suzuki and Yamaha, or the more functional 'Bahnstormers' created by BMW and since duplicated in the form of Honda's Pan European ST1100 and Kawasaki's 1000GTR.

Then there are the street cruisers, led by the awesome Yamaha V-Max, the new Yamaha TDM850 and models such as Suzuki's VX800. They have the performance and the style that draws the crowd. The most popular leisure bikes are the dual purpose all-terrain machines. Brash styling, which combines the strong outdoor looks of the Enduro with the sophistication of the road bike, has created models like Honda's Transalp, Kawasaki's KLE500, Cagiva's Elefant, Suzuki's DR800S and Yamaha's Super Tenéré. These bikes have transformed the basic trail model with its bare frame, thin knobbly tyres, kick starting and feeble 6 volt lighting.

Top of the range for most manufacturers are the race-replica sports models, featuring the latest ideas tested on the Grand Prix circuits of the world. This edition shows the increasing popularity of mid-range models in Works racer-styling. In general, the scaled-down versions are cheaper to buy and to insure than the full-size replicas. Typical examples are Kawasaki's ZXR400, Yamaha's FZR400, Suzuki's RGV250 and Honda's NSR125R and VFR400R3. The 1990s seem likely to witness a re-appraisal of the importance of power and performance to motorcycle design, with greater emphasis being placed on safety and efficiency features.

For commuting, the lightweight step-thru remains a best-seller but there has been a recent upsurge of popularity in scooters. Unchanged for many years, the scooter is being re-packaged as an ideal form of city runabout. Piaggio dominates the scooter market but the Honda CN250 combines looks, size and a unique feet-forward riding position.

An indication of what may be the styling feature of the decade is provided in part by the Bimota Tesi and a prototype by Yamaha named Morpho. These are motorcycles that are adjustable and can be set up for individual riding positions; bikes capable of adapting to their riders. Another nineties look is provided by the 'Retro bikes', such as the Suzuki GSX1100G and the Kawasaki Zephyrs, which match timeless styling features with tested, mechanical simplicity for the traditionalist.

Technically, the most interesting challenge for the nineties will be finding ways to make biking more environmentally friendly. So far, developments have included agreeing voluntary power output limits (100 bhp in Germany, 125 bhp in the United Kingdom), attempts to improve fuel efficiency through computerised engine management systems, stricter exhaust noise controls and the introduction of compulsory training schemes. The next step will be fitting catalytic converters to bikes.

The 'cleaning and greening' of bikes is expected to add about ten per cent to prices and may mean some power losses. Emission controls, already mandatory in North America, are expected to be a requirement in Europe by 1993. Catalytic converters are designed to reduce unburnt hydro-carbons and residue oxides of nitrogen and carbon in exhaust gases. The more expensive bikes (like BMW's K1) employ active converters with exhaust sensors linked to engine management systems, to ensure optimum fuel/air mixtures are being used at all speeds. The uncontrolled option uses a honeycomb catalyst chamber positioned in the exhaust pipe.

The Anti-lock Braking Systems (ABS) represents the main safety development on bikes since disc brakes and better-gripping tyre compounds improved stopping efficiency in the 1970s. BMW pioneered ABS on motorcycles and Yamaha has become the first Japanese manufacturer to fit the system to a production machine. ABS uses wheel sensors linked to an electronic control unit that can react faster than the average rider to over-braking and any impending wheel lock-up.

The costs and complexity of biking continue to soar, boosted by the race-derived high technology features used to dazzle buyers. Even 50 cc machines feature Works-racer, aluminium beam frames, upside down, anti-dive front forks, banana-shaped swinging arms, single shock rear suspensions, bean-can exhausts and dramatic graphics on the fully-enclosed bodywork. The race pack options on the full-sized replicas add further elements, such as flat slide carbs with accelerator pumps, close ratio gearboxes, four-piston caliper floating brakes and low-profile radial tyres. Weight-saving measures include using magnesium for engine covers, slimming crankshafts and fitting cast alloy wheels with hollow hubs. The result is fast, eye-catching and adrenalin-pumping.

Although some of the 'Retro' models, such as the Honda Revere and the Suzuki Bandit, go naked in the traditional fashion, the general trend is to an all-enveloping bodywork style. Fully enclosed fairings are designed to reduce air drag on performance and to offer the rider sensible protection from the elements. The wide expanses of metal or plastic provide a surface for the startling graphics and colours which are a feature of many models today. However, it has been necessary to develop effective air ducting, both to reduce air turbulence around the rider's space and to ensure a cool flow to brakes and carburettors.

This book has been made possible by the helpful co-operation of motorcycle manufacturers around the world and my thanks are extended for this assistance. While every effort has been made to ensure the book's accuracy, it is not possible to guarantee all the specifications quoted, as manufacturers always reserve the right to alter model details without notice. Moreover, model specifications vary from country to country. The motorcycles featured in this seventh edition are from the 1990/91 ranges and are, in most cases, models sold in the United Kingdom and Europe.

Robert Croucher

Technical Specifications Explained

How to use this book

Model: Manufacturers identify each model in their bike range by a code of letters and numbers; sometimes a model also gets a name. These codes describe the type of bike, its engine capacity and may indicate a special feature or the year of its introduction. The codes are not standardised and model labels such as 'Supersport', 'GP' or 'Special' may mean different things to each manufacturer. Names are also used to create an image for new engineering developments. Thus all Harley-Davidson models now run the 'Evolution' engine and the advanced design technology of Yamaha's FZ range is labelled 'Genesis'.

Engine: Motorcycle engines come in single- or multi-cylinder form with a two- or four-stroke combustion cycle. Two-strokes are further classified by their fuel mixture intake system as reed or rotary-disc valve. Four-stroke engines are described by their valve actuating mechanism as overhead (ohv), single (sohc), or double (dohc) overhead camshafts. Two valves per cylinder have been customary for motorcycle engines but the quest for better performance has led to four and even five valves being fitted (three inlet and two exhaust) to speed gas-flow rate and to improve combustion efficiency. A four-valve in-line four engine can also be described as a 16-valve motor.

Single cylinder engines normally sit vertically in the bike frame although mopeds may have horizontally placed blocks. Multi-cylinder configurations can be in-line across the frame, in a vee or a flat formation to create twins, triples, fours and even sixes. The engines of sports bikes are typically inclined forward at 45 degrees to improve weight distribution for better handling. 'LC' indicates an engine with liquid cooling by water jacket and radiator. Suzuki has pioneered oil cooling for engines but most machines are still air-cooled. Powervalves tune exhaust performance in order to improve throttle response and increase pulling power.

Capacity: This is the cubic content of the cylinder(s), measured in centimetres. This measure of engine size may be significant for taxation, insurance and safety legislation purposes. Bikes range in size, mostly from 49 cc to over 1 400 cc.

Bore × Stroke: A measure in millimetres of the relationship between the cylinder head diameter and the length of the piston working within it. Modern motorcycles are often short stroke and square. Long stroke thumping is more characteristic of big touring bikes and the large capacity street-enduro machines.

Compression ratio: A measure of the compression of the fuel/air mixture in each cylinder as the piston rises before ignition. A high-compression engine is one with a ratio of 9:1 or more.

Carburettor: This meters fuel and air to the engine. The number of carbs, their choke-size diameter and the make are given. The carburettor may be of the piston slide or constant velocity (cv) type. Suzuki has developed the *Slingshot* design which combines the best features of a flat slide and a round slide carb to maintain rapid engine response. Some bikes now use fuel injection as part of computerised engine-management systems.

Maximum power: The brake horsepower (bhp) and the engine speed (rpm) at which maximum power output is achieved are given. The figure can vary widely with the method used to measure it. Most of the figures quoted in this book are to the German DIN standard, which measures the net output of the engine at the rear wheel under normal use conditions with pumps and generators working. The actual figure quoted may reflect a voluntary power limitation agreement within a country rather than the actual output of the engine. Learner category machines may be restricted by legislation.

Starting: Most bikes are fired up by push-button electric starters. Some bikes, particularly light trail machines, retain the kick-operated crank and mopeds may be started using pedals.

Transmission: The number of gears and the method of final drive to the rear wheel are given. Most bikes use a wet, multi-plate clutch to engage and disengage engine drive. Some machines are fitted with belt drive rather than conventional link chains. Mopeds and scooters often use centrifugal clutches to provide a completely automatic drive.

Electrics: A bike's electrical supply usually comes from a 12 v system. The ignition timing is commonly electronic and maintenance-free. The new, micro-controlled digital systems provide optimum ignition timing at every engine rpm. The battery capacity is described in ampere-hours (Ah). Some lightweights still use a simple 6 v system with direct charging from a flywheel magneto. They may have a small dry-cell battery to supply lighting when stationary.

Frame: Normally this is a strong tubular steel frame formed into a single or double cradle. High-performance machines feature race-derived, wrap round, reinforced aluminium-alloy frames like the Deltabox used for Yamaha superbikes. Some bikes have the engine suspended from a pressed-steel beam acting as a stressed member. Scooters often feature integral monocoque body construction.

Suspension: The front suspension is usually by telescopic fork with compression and rebound damping by coil springs and hydraulic pressure. Some of the bigger bikes supplement this system with infinitely variable air pressure arrangements. Anti-dive systems are used to further control the compression damping of the front fork under the load of severe braking. A recent trend is to fit the front fork upside down. This has been track-tested and helps to give improved front-end rigidity.

The conventional rear suspension set-up employs a swinging arm with twin hydraulic shock absorbers. For lightness the swinging arm is often made from box-section aluminium. The rear single shock system, designed originally for motocross racers, is widely used on road bikes. Monoshock trade names include Honda's *Pro-Link*, Kawasaki's *Uni-Trak*, Suzuki's

Full-Floater and Yamaha's *Monocross*. Both the spring pre-load and the damping characteristics of monoshock systems may be adjustable to take account of extra weight on the bike or particular road conditions. Some models feature piggyback-style, remote-reservoir hydraulic shock absorbers, borrowed from the motocross racers.

Brakes: Braking can be by drums or discs. The drilled disc is now almost universal. Bigger machines usually have twin front discs which have four or twin piston calipers to generate maximum braking force. Their brake discs float via rollers on the brake disc carrier to resist heat-related distortion, to eliminate brake squeal and to ensure that the full area of the brake lining is always available for high-performance stopping. The ABS fitted on BMW and Yamaha machines controls wheel lockup and provides smooth braking operation while minimising the braking distances required, particularly on wet and slippery road surfaces.

Tyres: Traditionally, motorcycle wheels were wire-spoked, but most bikes now feature cast aluminium, hollow-spoke wheels to reduce the unsprung weight of the machine and to improve suspension performance. Tyres, often radial and tubeless, are ribbed at the front to give positive steering ability. The rear rubber is broader with a curved profile and deep, zig-zag treads to grip the road on cornering and for acceleration.

Tyre sizes are indicated in a variety of ways. A size of 3.50–18 indicates the tyre width and the wheel-rim diameter in inches. A tyre may also be described as 170/60ZR17, where the 170 measures the tyre width in millimetres, the 60 is a percentage and refers to the ratio between the height of the tyre and its width, and the 17 is the wheel-rim diameter in inches. The letters ZR indicate that the tyre is rated for high-speed riding. V and H are high-speed ratings and S is on standard road tyres. These speed ratings are based on correct inflation on the right rim size wheel and ridden within the designed load capacity of the bike.

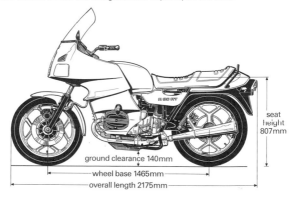

seat height 807mm

ground clearance 140mm

wheel base 1465mm

overall length 2175mm

Dimensions: Metric measures are given for each bike, as illustrated in the drawing of a BMW R80RT.

The 'Dry weight' figure provides a standard so that bikes can be compared regardless of any differences in fuel or oil capacity. The 'Fuel tank' figure is a maximum and usually includes several litres for reserve.

Performance: Most manufacturers are reluctant to provide performance figures for their motorcycles because what can be achieved clearly varies with the rider and the conditions under which the testing has been carried out. The examples used in this book are averages of published test results from the motorcycle press and should be read as approximate limits rather than absolute benchmarks. Fuel consumption figures, in particular, can be very misleading as they may have been obtained under conditions of steady, slow-speed running. The figures given are only a rough guide to what might be obtained under typical, mixed riding conditions. 7 l/100 km is equivalent to 40 mpg.

Features: Details of any special equipment fitted or available.

Note
... This indicates that information was not available when the book was published.

APRILIA (Italy)

Model: Pegaso 600

Engine: 4-str 4-valve single
Capacity: 562.1 cc
Bore × Stroke: 94 × 81 mm
Compression ratio: 9.4:1
Carburettor: 34 mm Dell'Orto
Maximum power: 46 bhp at
7 000 rpm
Starting: electric

Transmission: 5-speed chain

Electrics: 12 v electronic
ignition

Frame: Single beam with
removable cradle

Suspension: 38 mm upside
down fork with adjustable *APS*
rear monoshock

Brakes: 300 mm front disc and
220 mm rear disc

Tyres: Front is 100/90-19
Rear is 130/80-17

Dimensions:
Length: 2 210 mm
Width: 850 mm
Wheelbase: 1 505 mm
Clearance: 300 mm
Seat height: 910 mm
Dry weight: 148 kg
Fuel tank: 14.5 litres

Performance:
Top speed: 167 km/h
Fuel consumption: 4.3 l/100 km

Features: Half fairing and
engine bash-plate. Hand
protectors. For 1991 with 5-valve
650 cc engine.

Manufacturer: Aprilia S.p.A., via G. Galilei, 1, 30033 Noale (VE), Italy.

APRILIA (Italy)

Model: AF1 125 Futura

Engine: 2-str LC reed-valve single
Capacity: 124.7 cc
Bore × Stroke: 54 × 54.5 mm
Compression ratio: 13.6:1
Carburettor: 34 mm Dell'Orto
Maximum power: ...
Starting: electric

Transmission: 6-speed chain

Electrics: 12 v electronic ignition with 4 Ah battery

Frame: Double aluminium tube

Suspension: 38 mm upside down fork with adjustable 'APS' rear monoshock

Manufacturer: Aprilia S.p.A.

Brakes: 320 mm floating disc and 240 mm rear disc

Tyres: Front is 100/80-16
Rear is 130/70-17

Dimensions:
Length: 1 990 mm
Width: 615 mm
Wheelbase: 1 365 mm
Clearance: 130 mm
Seat height: 800 mm
Dry weight: 113 kg
Fuel tank: 14.5 litres

Performance:
Top speed: 168 km/h
Fuel consumption: 4.5 l/100 km

Features: Race track styling. Also available in 50 cc version.

APRILIA (Italy)

Model: Red Rose 125

Engine: 2-str LC reed-valve
single
Capacity: 124.7 cc
Bore × Stroke: 54 × 54.4 mm
Compression ratio: 14.2:1
Carburettor: 26 mm Dell'Orto
Maximum power: 27 bhp at
10 250 rpm
Starting: electric

Transmission: 6-speed chain

Electrics: 12 v electronic
ignition

Frame: Double tubular cradle

Suspension: 35 mm long travel
fork with twin adjustable rear
shocks

Manufacturer: Aprilia S.p.A.

Brakes: 260 mm floating disc
and 160 mm rear drum

Tyres: Front is 90/90-19
Rear is 130/90-16

Dimensions:
Length: 2 199 mm
Width: 775 mm
Wheelbase: 1 525 mm
Clearance: 130 mm
Seat height: 780 mm
Dry weight: 120 kg
Fuel tank: 12 litres

Performance:
Top speed: 132 km/h
Fuel consumption: 4 l/100 km

Features: Custom-style. Also in
50 cc version

BENELLI (Italy)

Model: 900 Sei

Engine: 4-str sohc in-line six
Capacity: 905.9 cc
Bore × Stroke: 60 × 53.4 mm
Compression ratio: 9.5:1
Carburettor: 3 × 24 mm Dell'Orto
Maximum power: 80 bhp at
8 400 rpm
Starting: electric

Transmission: 5-speed chain

Electrics: 12 v electronic
ignition with 28 Ah battery

Frame: Duplex tubular cradle

Suspension: Telescopic front
fork with twin adjustable rear
shocks

Brakes: 300 mm twin discs and
260 mm rear disc

Tyres: Front is 100/90V18
Rear is 120/90V18

Dimensions:
Length: 2 110 mm
Width: 690 mm
Wheelbase: 1 460 mm
Clearance: 150 mm
Seat height: 790 mm
Dry weight: 220 kg
Fuel tank: 16.5 litres

Performance:
Top speed: 218 km/h
Fuel consumption: 8 l/100 km

Features: Linked braking,
3-into-2 exhaust. Modern six
cylinder classic.

Manufacturer: GBM S.p.A., Chiusa di Ginestreto, 61100 Pesaro, Italy.

BENELLI (Italy)

Model: 125 Jarno

Engine: 2-str power-valve single
Capacity: 123.15 cc
Bore × Stroke: 56 × 50 mm
Compression ratio: 13.5:1
Carburettor: 28 mm Dell'Orto
Maximum power: 27 bhp at 9 800 rpm
Starting: electric

Transmission: 6-speed chain

Electrics: 12 v Motoplat ignition

Frame: Double lateral beam

Suspension: Telehydraulic front fork with rear monoshock system

Manufacturer: GBM S.p.A.

Brakes: 240 mm triple disc system

Tyres: Front is 100/80-16
Rear is 120/80-16

Dimensions:
Length: ...
Width: ...
Wheelbase: ...
Clearance: ...
Seat height: ...
Dry weight: 118 kg
Fuel tank: 20 litres

Performance:
Top speed: 150 km/h
Fuel consumption: ...

Features: Aluminium alloy frame. GP styling.

BENELLI (Italy)

Model: 125 BX

Engine: 2-str LC single
Capacity: 123.15 cc
Bore × Stroke: 56 × 50 mm
Compression ratio: 7:1
Carburettor: 24 mm Dell'Orto
Maximum power: 20 bhp at
8 000 rpm
Starting: kick

Transmission: 6-speed chain

Electrics: 12 v electronic
ignition with 7 Ah battery

Frame: Box section cradle

Suspension: Marzocchi air fork
with rear hydraulic monoshock

Manufacturer: GBM S.p.A.

Brakes: 260 mm shrouded front
disc and 125 mm drum

Tyres: Front is 2.75–21
Rear is 4.10–18

Dimensions:
Length: 1 860 mm
Width: 715 mm
Wheelbase: 1 220 mm
Clearance: 330 mm
Seat height: 850 mm
Dry weight: 105 kg
Fuel tank: 10 litres

Performance:
Top speed: 130 km/h
Fuel consumption: 3.3 l/100 km

Features: Rear carrier.

BETAMOTOR (Italy)

Model: Zero 260

Engine: 2-str LC reed-valve
single
Capacity: 260.7 cc
Bore × Stroke: 76 × 57.5 mm
Compression ratio: 10.6:1
Carburettor: 26 mm Dell'Orto
Maximum power: ...
Starting: kick

Transmission: 6-speed chain

Electrics: 12 v electronic
ignition

Frame: Aluminium diamond

Suspension: Reversed
telehydraulic fork with rear
monoshock system

Brakes: 185 mm front disc and
160 mm rear disc

Tyres: Front is 2.75–21
Rear is 4.00–18

Dimensions:
Length: 2 040 mm
Width: 830 mm
Wheelbase: 1 320 mm
Clearance: 350 mm
Seat height: 710 mm
Dry weight: 82 kg
Fuel tank: 4 litres

Performance:
Top speed: ...
Fuel consumption: ...

Features: World champion Trial
bike in 1990. Front disc protector.
Other models include the air-
cooled TR35 and Alp 240.

Manufacturer: Betamotor S.p.A., Pian dell'Isola, 72, 50067 Rignano
sull'Arno(FI), Italy.

BETAMOTOR (Italy)

Model: MX Enduro 50

Engine: 2-str LC reed-valve
single
Capacity: 49.86 cc
Bore × Stroke: 40 × 39.7 mm
Compression ratio: 11:1
Carburettor: 14–12 mm Dell'Orto
Maximum power: 1.5 bhp at
4 000 rpm
Starting: kick

Transmission: 3-speed chain

Electrics: electronic ignition

Frame: Tubular cradle

Suspension: Reversed
telehydraulic fork with rear
monoshock system

Manufacturer: Betamotor S.p.A.

Brakes: 220 mm disc front and
rear

Tyres: Front is 2.50–21
Rear is 3.50–18

Dimensions:
Length: 1 970 mm
Width: 800 mm
Wheelbase: 1 240 mm
Clearance: 330 mm
Seat height: 730 mm
Dry weight: 65 kg
Fuel tank: 7 litres

Performance:
Top speed: 40 km/h
Fuel consumption: 2 l/100 km

Features:

BETAMOTOR (Italy)

Model: Four XP 50

Engine: 2-str single
Capacity: 49.86 cc
Bore × Stroke: 40 × 39.7 mm
Compression ratio: 11:1
Carburettor: 14–12 mm Dell'Orto
Maximum power: 1.5 bhp at
4 000 rpm
Starting: kick

Transmission: 4-speed chain

Electrics: 12 v electronic
ignition

Frame: Pressed steel step-thru

Suspension: Telehydraulic
front fork with rear monoshock
system

Manufacturer: Betamotor S.p.A.

Brakes: 118 mm drums front
and rear

Tyres: Front is 2.75–16
Rear is 2.75–17

Dimensions:
Length: 1 780 mm
Width: ...
Wheelbase: 1 100 mm
Clearance: ...
Seat height: 860 mm
Dry weight: 64 kg
Fuel tank: 7 litres

Performance:
Top speed: 40 km/h
Fuel consumption: 2 l/100 km

Features: Rear carrier. Similar
models are Four RV and Twin
Four 50.

BIMOTA (Italy)

Model: Dieci

Engine: 4-str LC dohc in-line
Yamaha four
Capacity: 1 002 cc
Bore × Stroke: 75.5 × 56 mm
Compression ratio: 12:1
Carburettor: 4 × 38 mm Mikuni
Maximum power: 149 bhp at
10 000 rpm
Starting: electric

Transmission: 5-speed chain

Electrics: 12 v digital ignition

Frame: Aluminium diamond

Suspension: Upside down
telehydraulic front fork with rear
monoshock

Brakes: Twin 300 mm front
discs and rear 260 mm disc

Tyres: Front is 120/70ZR17
Rear is 180/55ZR17

Dimensions:
Length: 2 100 mm
Width: 680 mm
Wheelbase: 1 420 mm
Clearance: 160 mm
Seat height: 845 mm
Dry weight: 185 kg
Fuel tank: 20 litres

Performance:
Top speed: 280 km/h
Fuel consumption: 7 l/100 km

Features: Full fairing. Brembo
brakes. Celebrates 10th
anniversary of Bimota's
collaboration with Yamaha.

Manufacturer: Bimota S.p.A., via Giaccaglia, 38, 47037 Rimini, Italy.

BIMOTA (Italy)

Model: Tesi 1D

Engine: Ducati 4-str LC dohc 4-valve 90° vee-twin
Capacity: 906 cc
Bore × Stroke: 92 × 68 mm
Compression ratio: 11:1
Carburettor: injection
Maximum power: 113 bhp at 8 500 rpm
Starting: electric

Transmission: 6-speed chain

Electrics: 12 v digital ignition

Frame: Aluminium alloy diamond

Suspension: Swinging arm with single shocker front and rear

Manufacturer: Bimota S.p.A.

Brakes: Twin 300 mm floating discs and 230 mm rear disc

Tyres: Front is 120/70ZR17
Rear is 180/55ZR17 tubeless

Dimensions:
Length: 2 030 mm
Width: 730 mm
Wheelbase: 1 410 mm
Clearance: 130 mm
Seat height: 780 mm
Dry weight: 188 kg
Fuel tank: 20 litres

Performance:
Top speed: 250 km/h
Fuel consumption: 6 l/100 km

Features: Also in 851 cc stock form. New technology model. Integrated engine management system. Adjustable frame. Hub-centre steering.

BIMOTA (Italy)

Model: Bellaria 600

Engine: Yamaha 4-str LC dohc
in-line four
Capacity: 599 cc
Bore × Stroke: 59 × 54.8 mm
Compression ratio: 9.7:1
Carburettor: 4 × 32 mm Mikuni
Maximum power: 95 bhp at
10 500 rpm
Starting: electric

Transmission: 6-speed chain

Electrics: 12 v electronic
ignition

Frame: Bimota aluminium alloy

Suspension: Upside down
telehydraulic fork with rear
monoshock

Manufacturer: Bimota S.p.A.

Brakes: Twin 300 mm floating
discs and rear 230 mm disc

Tyres: Front is 120/70ZR17
Rear is 160/60ZR17 tubeless

Dimensions:
Length: 2 060 mm
Width: 630 mm
Wheelbase: 1 375 mm
Clearance: 160 mm
Seat height: 845 mm
Dry weight: 179 kg
Fuel tank: 20 litres

Performance:
Top speed: 240 km/h
Fuel consumption: 4.4 l/100 km

Features: Bimota's first two
seater. Digital instrumentation.
Twin headlights.

BMW (Germany)

Model: K1

Engine: 4-str LC dohc 4-valve
flat four
Capacity: 987 cc
Bore × Stroke: 67 × 70 mm
Compression ratio: 11:1
Carburettor: injection
Maximum power: 100 bhp at
8 000 rpm
Starting: electric

Transmission: 5-speed with
shaft drive

Electrics: 12 v electronic
ignition with 25 Ah battery

Frame: Tubular space frame

Suspension: Marzocchi front
fork with rear *Paralever* system

Brakes: 305 mm twin discs with
285 mm rear disc

Tyres: Front is 120/70VR17
Rear is 160/60VR18 tubeless

Dimensions:
Length: 2 230 mm
Width: 760 mm
Wheelbase: 1 565 mm
Clearance: 160 mm
Seat height: 780 mm
Dry weight: 215 kg
Fuel tank: 22 litres

Performance:
Top speed: over 230 km/h
Fuel consumption: 5 l/100 km

Features: Sports version of the
K100RS. Catalytic converter. ABS
anti-lock braking option. Car type
engine management system.
Central locking.

Manufacturer: BMW Motorrad AG, 8000 München 45, Germany.

BMW (Germany)

Model: K 100 LT

Engine: 4-str dohc LC flat four
Capacity: 987 cc
Bore × Stroke: 67 × 70 mm
Compression ratio: 10.2:1
Carburettor: injection
Maximum power: 90 bhp at
8 000 rpm
Starting: electric

Transmission: 5-speed with
shaft drive

Electrics: 12 v electronic
ignition with 25 Ah battery

Frame: Tubular space frame
with engine acting as a
loadbearing component

Suspension: Telescopic front
fork with rear *Monolever* system

Manufacturer: BMW AG

Brakes: 285 mm triple slotted
disc system

Tyres: Front is 100/90V18
Rear is 130/90V17

Dimensions:
Length: 2 220 mm
Width: 916 mm
Wheelbase: 1 511 mm
Clearance: 175 mm
Seat height: 810 mm
Dry weight: 239 kg
Fuel tank: 22 litres

Performance:
Top speed: 215 km/h
Fuel consumption: 5 l/100 km

Features: Aerodynamic sports-
touring fairing, luggage rack and
topcase. ABS anti-lock braking
option. Also in Limited Edition
version.

BMW (Germany)

Model: K 100 RS

Engine: 4-str LC dohc flat four
Capacity: 987 cc
Bore × Stroke: 67 × 70 mm
Compression ratio: 11:1
Carburettor: injection
Maximum power: 100 bhp at
8 000 rpm
Starting: electric

Transmission: 5-speed with
shaft drive

Electrics: 12 v digital ignition
with 25 Ah battery

Frame: Tubular space frame
with engine acting as loadbearing
component

Suspension: Telescopic front
forks with rear *Paralever* system

Manufacturer: BMW AG.

Brakes: Twin 305 mm front
discs and 285 mm rear disc

Tyres: Front is 120/70VR17
Rear is 160/60VR18 tubeless

Dimensions:
Length: 2 230 mm
Width: 800 mm
Wheelbase: 1 564 mm
Clearance: 175 mm
Seat height: 800 mm
Dry weight: 229 kg
Fuel tank: 22 litres

Performance:
Top speed: 220 km/h
Fuel consumption: 5 l/100 km

Features: Touring full fairing.
Central locking. ABS system.

BMW (Germany)

Model: R 100 RS

Engine: 4-str ohv flat twin
Capacity: 980 cc
Bore × Stroke: 94 × 70.6 mm
Compression ratio: 8.45:1
Carburettor: 2 × 32 mm Bing
Maximum power: 60 bhp at
6 500 rpm
Starting: electric

Transmission: 5-speed with
shaft drive

Electrics: 12 v electronic
ignition with 30 Ah battery

Frame: Duplex tubular cradle

Suspension: Telescopic front
forks with rear *Monolever* system

Manufacturer: BMW AG.

Brakes: Twin 285 mm discs
with rear 200 mm drum

Tyres: Front is 90/90–18H
Rear is 120/90–18H

Dimensions:
Length: 2 175 mm
Width: 800 mm
Wheelbase: 1 447 mm
Clearance: 125 mm
Seat height: 807 mm
Dry weight: 207 kg
Fuel tank: 22 litres

Performance:
Top speed: 185 km/h
Fuel consumption: 6 l/100 km

Features: Oil cooler, sports
fairing. Classic model first
introduced in 1976. Low noise
level exhaust system.

BMW (Germany)

Model: R 100 GS Paris-Dakar

Engine: 4-str ohv flat twin
Capacity: 980 cc
Bore × Stroke: 94 × 70.6 mm
Compression ratio: 8.5:1
Carburettor: 2 × 40 mm Bing
Maximum power: 60 bhp at
6 500 rpm
Starting: electric

Transmission: 5-speed with
shaft drive

Electrics: 12 v electronic
ignition with 25 Ah battery

Frame: Duplex tubular cradle

Suspension: Telescopic front
fork with rear *Paralever* system

Manufacturer: BMW AG.

Brakes: 285 mm twin discs and
rear 200 mm drum

Tyres: Front is 90/90–21T
Rear is 130/80–17T

Dimensions:
Length: 2 290 mm
Width: 1 000 mm
Wheelbase: 1 513 mm
Clearance: 200 mm
Seat height: 850 mm
Dry weight: 192 kg
Fuel tank: 35 litres

Performance:
Top speed: 180 km/h
Fuel consumption: 6.4 l/100 km

Features: Solo seat, large
luggage rack, engine protection,
Handlebar mounted fairing. Also
standard R100GS version.

BMW (Germany)

Model: R80 GS

Engine: 4-str flat twin
Capacity: 798 cc
Bore × Stroke: 84.8 × 70.6 mm
Compression ratio: 8.2:1
Carburettor: 2 × 32 mm Bing
Maximum power: 50 bhp at
6 500 rpm
Starting: electric

Transmission: 5-speed shaft
drive

Electrics: 12 v electronic
ignition with 25 Ah battery

Frame: Duplex tubular cradle

Suspension: Telescopic front
forks with rear *Paralever* single
swinging arm

Manufacturer: BMW AG

Brakes: 285 mm front disc and
200 mm rear drum

Tyres: Front is 90/90–21F
Rear is 130/80–17T

Dimensions:
Length: 2 290 mm
Width: 1 000 mm
Wheelbase: 1 513 mm
Clearance: 200 mm
Seat height: 850 mm
Dry weight: 192 kg
Fuel tank: 24 litres

Performance:
Top speed: 168 km/h
Fuel consumption: 6 l/100 km

Features: New cockpit fairing
on the 10th anniversary of its
introduction.

BMW (Germany)

Model: K 75 S

Engine: 4-str LC dohc flat triple
Capacity: 740 cc
Bore × Stroke: 67 × 70 mm
Compression ratio: 11:1
Carburettor: injection
Maximum power: 75 bhp at
8 500 rpm
Starting: electric

Transmission: 5-speed with
shaft drive

Electrics: 12 v electronic
ignition with 25 Ah battery

Frame: Tubular space frame
with the engine as a loadbearing
component

Suspension: Telescopic front
forks with rear *Monolever* system

Manufacturer: BMW AG.

Brakes: 285 mm triple slotted
disc system

Tyres: Front is 100/90V18
Rear is 130/90V17 tubeless

Dimensions:
Length: 2 220 mm
Width: 810 mm
Wheelbase: 1 516 mm
Clearance: 175 mm
Seat height: 810 mm
Dry weight: 214 kg
Fuel tank: 21 litres

Performance:
Top speed: 210 km/h
Fuel consumption: 5 l/100 km

Features: Bosch LE Jetronic
fuel injection, frame fitted sports
fairing and engine spoiler. ABS
anti-lock brakes optional and in
1991 will be available with
catalytic converter.

CAGIVA (Italy)

Model: Elefant 900I.E.

Engine: 4-str desmodromic valve 90° vee-twin
Capacity: 904 cc
Bore × Stroke: 92 × 68 mm
Compression ratio: 9.2:1
Carburettor: Fuel injection
Maximum power: 68 bhp at 8 000 rpm
Starting: electric

Transmission: 6-speed chain

Electrics: 12 v electronic with 16 Ah battery

Frame: Box section single tube

Suspension: Telehydraulic leading link with rear *Soft-Damp* monoshock

Brakes: 296 mm floating disc and 240 mm rear disc

Tyres: Front is 100/90–19
Rear is 140/80–17

Dimensions:
Length: 2 295 mm
Width: 860 mm
Wheelbase: 1 570 mm
Clearance: 256 mm
Seat height: 896 mm
Dry weight: 188 kg
Fuel tank: 24 litres

Performance:
Top speed: 200 km/h
Fuel consumption: 5 l/100 km

Features: Twin headlight fairing, rear carrier, engine bash plate and hand guards. Also in Lucky Explorer colours.

Manufacturer: Cagiva Motor S.p.A., via G. Macchi, 144, 21100 Schiranna-Varese, Italy.

CAGIVA (Italy)

Model: T4 500 E

Engine: 4-str four-valve single
Capacity: 451 cc
Bore × Stroke: 94 × 65 mm
Compression ratio: 9:1
Carburettor: 40 mm Bing
Maximum power: 40 bhp at
7 000 rpm
Starting: electric and kick

Transmission: 5-speed chain

Electrics: 12 v electronic
ignition with 14 Ah battery

Frame: Single tube cradle

Suspension: Telehydraulic
leading link fork with rear *Soft-
Damp* monoshock

Brakes: 240 mm floating disc
and rear 130 mm drum

Tyres: Front is 90/90–21
Rear is 120/90–17

Dimensions:
Length: 2 185 mm
Width: 820 mm
Wheelbase: 1 440 mm
Clearance: 280 mm
Seat height: 910 mm
Dry weight: 149 kg
Fuel tank: 24 litres

Performance:
Top speed: 150 km/h
Fuel consumption: 4 l/100 km

Features: Rear carrier and
headlight guard. Also as lighter
R-model.

Manufacturer: Cagiva Motor S.p.A.

CAGIVA (Italy)

Model: T4 350 R

Engine: 4-str sohc four-valve single
Capacity: 343.3 cc
Bore × Stroke: 82 × 65 mm
Compression ratio: 9.5:1
Carburettor: 34 mm Dell'Orto
Maximum power: 34 bhp at 7 500 rpm
Starting: kick

Transmission: 5-speed chain

Electrics: 12 v electronic ignition with 3 Ah battery

Frame: Single tube cradle

Suspension: Telehydraulic leading link fork with rear *Soft-Damp* monoshock

Manufacturer: Cagiva Motor S.p.A.

Brakes: 240 floating disc and 130 mm rear drum

Tyres: Front is 90/90–21
Rear is 120/90–17

Dimensions:
Length: 2 185 mm
Width: 820 mm
Wheelbase: 1 440 mm
Clearance: 315 mm
Seat height: 935 mm
Dry weight: 135 kg
Fuel tank: 12 litres

Performance:
Top speed: 135 km/h
Fuel consumption: 5 l/100 km

Features: E-model has electric start.

CAGIVA (Italy)

Model: N 90 125

Engine: 2-str LC reed-valve single
Capacity: 124.6 cc
Bore × Stroke: 56 × 50.6 mm
Compression ratio: 6.3:1
Carburettor: 28 mm Dell'Orto
Maximum power: 31 bhp at 9 000 rpm
Starting: electric

Transmission: 7-speed chain

Electrics: 12 v CDI ignition with 9 Ah battery

Frame: Single tube cradle

Suspension: Upside down telehydraulic fork with rear 'Soft-Damp' monoshock

Manufacturer: Cagiva Motor S.p.A.

Brakes: 230 mm shrouded disc and 220 mm rear disc

Tyres: Front is 80/90–21
Rear is 120/80–17

Dimensions:
Length: 2 040 mm
Width: 820 mm
Wheelbase: 1 375 mm
Clearance: 320 mm
Seat height: 880 mm
Dry weight: 129 kg
Fuel tank: 14 litres

Performance:
Top speed: 140 km/h
Fuel consumption: 4 l/100 km

Features: Twin headlight fairing with engine protector and hand guards

CAGIVA (Italy)

Model: Mito

Engine: 2-str LC reed-valve single
Capacity: 124.6 cc
Bore × Stroke: 56 × 50.6 mm
Compression ratio: 6.3:1
Carburettor: 28 mm Dell'Orto
Maximum power: 31 bhp at 10 000 rmp
Starting: electric

Transmission: 7-speed chain

Electrics: 12 v CDI ignition with 9 Ah battery

Frame: Aluminium beam type

Suspension: Telehydraulic fork with anti-dive and rear *Soft-Damp* monoshock

Manufacturer: Cagiva Motor S.p.A.

Brakes: 320 mm Brembo disc and 230 mm rear disc

Tyres: Front is 100/80–17
Rear is 140/70–17

Dimensions:
Length: 2 000 mm
Width: 760 mm
Wheelbase: 1 380 mm
Clearance: 150 mm
Seat height: 770 mm
Dry weight: 121 kg
Fuel tank: 18 litres

Performance:
Top speed: 160 km/h
Fuel consumption: 4.5 l/100 km

Features: Full fairing with twin headlights. Also as unfaired model.

CAGIVA (Italy)

Model: Freccia 125 C12R

Engine: 2-str LC reed-valve single
Capacity: 124.6 cc
Bore × Stroke: 56 × 50.6 mm
Compression ratio: 6.3:1
Carburettor: 28 mm Dell'Orto
Maximum power: 31 bhp at 10 000 rpm
Starting: electric

Transmission: 7-speed chain

Electrics: 12 v CDI ignition with 9 Ah battery

Frame: Box section twin beam

Suspension: Telehydraulic fork with anti-dive and rear *Soft-Damp* monoshock

Manufacturer: Cagiva Motor S.p.A.

Brakes: 298 mm front disc and rear 240 mm disc

Tyres: Front is 100/80–16
Rear is 130/70–17

Dimensions:
Length: 1 960 mm
Width: 650 mm
Wheelbase: 1 370 mm
Clearance: 135 mm
Seat height: 770 mm
Dry weight: 125 kg
Fuel tank: 14 litres

Performance:
Top speed: 160 km/h
Fuel consumption: 4.5 l/100 km

Features: Slippery fairing with streamlined front mudguard. Electronic exhaust port system.

CAGIVA (Italy)

Model: K7

Engine: 2-str LC reed-valve
single
Capacity: 124.6 cc
Bore × Stroke: 56 × 50 mm
Compression ratio: 5.9:1
Carburettor: 34 mm Dell'Orto
Maximum power: . . .
Starting: kick

Transmission: 7-speed chain

Electrics: 12 v CDI ignition
with 4 Ah battery

Frame: Single tube cradle

Suspension: Telehydraulic
leading link fork and rear *Soft-
Damp* monoshock

Brakes: 260 mm Brembo disc
and rear 220 mm disc

Tyres: Front is 90/90–21
Rear is 120/80–18

Dimensions:
Length: 2 100 mm
Width: 870 mm
Wheelbase: 1 390 mm
Clearance: 360 mm
Seat height: 940 mm
Dry weight: 120 kg
Fuel tank: 14 litres

Performance:
Top speed: 135 km/h
Fuel consumption: 4 l/100 km

Features: New style off-road
machine with lights and
instrumentation.

Manufacturer: Cagiva Motor S.p.A.

CAGIVA (Italy)

Model: Cocis 75

Engine: 2-str LC reed-valve single
Capacity: 49.9 cc
Bore × Stroke: 46.5 × 44 mm
Compression ratio: 6.7:1
Carburettor: 17 mm Dell'Orto
Maximum power: 9 bhp at 8 250 rpm
Starting: electric

Transmission: 6-speed chain

Electrics: 12 v CDI ignition with 5 Ah battery

Frame: Single tube cradle

Suspension: Upside down telehydraulic fork and rear *Soft-Damp* monoshock

Manufacturer: Cagiva Motor S.p.A.

Brakes: 230 mm front disc and 220 mm rear disc

Tyres: Front is 2.75–21
Rear is 4.10–18

Dimensions:
Length: 2 050 mm
Width: 820 mm
Wheelbase: 1 350 mm
Clearance: 305 mm
Seat height: 880 mm
Dry weight: 102 kg
Fuel tank: 9 litres

Performance:
Top speed: 95 km/h
Fuel consumption: 4 l/100 km

Features: Shrouded front disc, hand guards and twin headlight fairing. Also as 6 bhp Cocis 50 version.

CASAL (Portugal)

Model: RZ 50

Engine: 2-str LC single
Capacity: 49.9 cc
Bore × Stroke: 40 × 39.7 mm
Compression ratio: 8.5:1
Carburettor: 19 mm Bing
Maximum power: 8.5 bhp at
9 000 rpm
Starting: kick

Transmission: 6-speed chain

Electrics: 6 v flywheel magneto
ignition

Frame: Tubular cradle

Suspension: Telescopic front
fork with twin adjustable rear
shocks

Brakes: 220 mm front disc and
118 mm rear drum

Tyres: Front is 2.50–17
Rear is 2.75–17

Dimensions:
Length: 1 830 mm
Width: 710 mm
Wheelbase: 1 230 mm
Clearance: 130 mm
Seat height: 760 mm
Dry weight: 83 kg
Fuel tank: 10 litres

Performance:
Top speed: 98 km/h
Fuel consumption: 3.2 l/100 km

Features: Handlebar-mounted
fairing

Manufacturer: Metalurgia Casal S.A.R.L., Apartado 83- 3801 Aveiro,
Portugal.

CASAL (Portugal)

Model: Super Boss K168T

Engine: 2-str single
Capacity: 49.9 cc
Bore × Stroke: 40 × 39.7 mm
Compression ratio: 8.5:1
Carburettor: 17 mm Bing
Maximum power: 5.3 bhp at
7 500 rpm
Starting: kick

Transmission: 4-speed chain

Electrics: 6 v flywheel magneto
ignition

Frame: Tubular steel

Suspension: Telescopic front
fork with twin adjustable rear
shocks

Brakes: 140 mm drums front
and rear

Tyres: Front is 3.00–16
Rear is 3.25–16

Dimensions:
Length: 1 870 mm
Width: 720 mm
Wheelbase: 1 250 mm
Clearance: 140 mm
Seat height: 750 mm
Dry weight: 76 kg
Fuel tank: 12 litres

Performance:
Top speed: 80 km/h
Fuel consumption: 3.1 l/100 km

Features: The Boss model
develops 2.5 bhp.

Manufacturer: Metalurgia Casal S.A.R.L.

CZM (Czechoslovakia)

Model: CZ125

Engine: 2-str single
Capacity: 123.7 cc
Bore × Stroke: 52 × 58 mm
Compression ratio: 8.6:1
Carburettor: Jikov
Maximum power: 11.5 bhp at
5 750 rpm
Starting: kick

Transmission: 4-speed chain

Electrics: 6 v dynamo and coil
ignition

Frame: Tubular cradle

Suspension: Telescopic front
fork with twin adjustable rear
shocks

Brakes: 160 mm drums front
and rear

Tyres: Front is 2.75–18
Rear is 3.00–18

Dimensions:
Length: 2 020 mm
Width: 660 mm
Wheelbase: 1 330 mm
Clearance: 120 mm
Seat height: 775 mm
Dry weight: 112 kg
Fuel tank: 12 litres

Performance:
Top speed: 85 km/h
Fuel consumption: 3 l/100 km

Features: Petroil lubrication,
tool kit and tyre inflator. Also in
175 cc version. Fitted with
cockpit fairing.

Manufacturer: CZM Strakonice, Czechoslovakia.

DERBI (Spain)

Model: FDS Savannah

Engine: 2-str single
Capacity: 48.8 cc
Bore × Stroke: 38 × 43 mm
Compression ratio: 10.5:1
Carburettor: 12 mm Dell'Orto
Maximum power: 2.5 bhp at
5 500 rpm
Starting: kick

Transmission: 4-speed chain

Electrics: 6 v Motoplat ignition

Frame: Tubular cradle

Suspension: Telehydraulic
front fork with rear Derbi-Track
monoshock

Brakes: 220 mm shrouded disc
and rear 130 mm drum

Tyres: Front is 2.75–21
Rear is 3.50–18

Dimensions:
Length: 1 985 mm
Width: 830 mm
Wheelbase: 1 300 mm
Clearance: 310 mm
Seat height: 895 mm
Dry weight: 80 kg
Fuel tank: 11 litres

Performance:
Top speed: 50 km/h
Fuel consumption: 3 l/100 km

Features:

Manufacturer: Derbi Nacional Motor SA., 08100 Martorelles,
Barcelona, Spain.

DERBI (Spain)

Model: Variant 50

Engine: 2-str single
Capacity: 49.9 cc
Bore × Stroke: 39.8 × 40 mm
Compression ratio: 10:1
Carburettor: 12 mm Dell'Orto
Maximum power: 2.85 bhp at
6 500 rpm
Starting: electric

Transmission: Single speed
automatic

Electrics: 6 v Motoplat ignition

Frame: Pressed steel step-thru

Suspension: Telescopic front
fork with twin rear shocks

Brakes: 105 mm drums front
and rear

Tyres: 2.50–17 front and rear

Dimensions:
Length: 1 780 mm
Width: 690 mm
Wheelbase: 1 200 mm
Clearance: 140 mm
Seat height: 770 mm
Dry weight: 60 kg
Fuel tank: 3.3 litres

Performance:
Top speed: 50 km/h
Fuel consumption: 2.5 l/100 km

Features: Fully-enclosed chain,
cast wheels, cockpit fairing.

Manufacturer: Derbi Nacional Motor SA.

DUCATI (Italy)

Model: Paso 907 I.E.

Engine: 4-str LC ohc Desmo-valve 90° vee-twin
Capacity: 904 cc
Bore × Stroke: 92 × 68 mm
Compression ratio: 9.2:1
Carburettor: Injection
Maximum power: 84 bhp at 8 400 rpm
Starting: electric

Transmission: 6-speed chain

Electrics: 12 v electronic ignition with 19 Ah battery

Frame: Box section double cradle

Suspension: Oleo telehydraulic front fork with anti-dive and rear *Soft-Damp*

Brakes: Twin 300 mm Brembo discs and rear 245 mm disc

Tyres: Front is 120/70ZR17
Rear is 170/60ZR17

Dimensions:
Length: 2 090 mm
Width: 700 mm
Wheelbase: 1 490 mm
Clearance: 170 mm
Seat height: 780 mm
Dry weight: 215 kg
Fuel tank: 21 litres

Performance:
Top speed: 230 km/h
Fuel consumption: 5.4 l/100 km

Features: Enclosed bodywork. Uses Desmodromic valve system.

Manufacturer: Ducati Meccanica S.p.A., via A Cavalieri Ducati, 3, 40100 Bologna, Italy.

DUCATI (Italy)

Model: 900 Supersport

Engine: 4-str LC ohc Desmo-
valve 90° vee-twin
Capacity: 904 cc
Bore × Stroke: 92 × 68 mm
Compression ratio: 9.2:1
Carburettor: 2 × 38 mm Mikuni
Maximum power: 84 bhp at
7 000 rpm
Starting: electric

Transmission: 6-speed chain

Electrics: 12 v electronic
ignition with 16 Ah battery

Frame: Tubular space frame

Suspension: Upside down
Showa fork with rear monoshock
system

Brakes: Twin 320 mm floating
discs and 245 mm rear disc

Tyres: Front is 120/70A59X17
Rear is 170/60M59X17

Dimensions:
Length: 2 030 mm
Width: 730 mm
Wheelbase: 1 410 mm
Clearance: 150 mm
Seat height: 780 mm
Dry weight: 186 kg
Fuel tank: 17.5 litres

Performance:
Top speed: 220 km/h
Fuel consumption: 5.8 l/100 km

Features: Half fairing, stainless
steel exhaust, oil cooler.

Manufacturer: Ducati Meccanica S.p.A.

DUCATI (Italy)

Model: 851 Sport

Engine: 4-str LC ohc Desmo-valve 90° vee-twin
Capacity: 888 cc
Bore × Stroke: 94 × 64 mm
Compression ratio: 11:1
Carburettor: Injection
Maximum power: 128 bhp at 10 500 rpm
Starting: electric

Transmission: 6-speed chain

Electrics: 12 v electronic ignition with 16 Ah battery

Frame: Chrome Molybdenum lattice

Suspension: Upside down Ohlins fork with rear monoshock system.

Brakes: Twin 320 mm floating discs and 245 mm rear disc

Tyres: Front is 120/70ZR17
Rear is 180/55ZR17

Dimensions:
Length: 2 000 mm
Width: 670 mm
Wheelbase: 1 430 mm
Clearance: 150 mm
Seat height: 760 mm
Dry weight: 188 kg
Fuel tank: 20 litres

Performance:
Top speed: 250 km/h
Fuel consumption: 5 l/100 km

Features: World Superbike version. Dual seat for road use.

Manufacturer: Ducati Meccanica S.p.A.

DUCATI (Italy)

Model: 851 Superbike

Engine: 4-str LC ohc Desmo-
valve 90° vee-twin
Capacity: 851 cc
Bore × Stroke: 92 × 64 mm
Compression ratio: 10.5:1
Carburettor: Injection
Maximum power: 105 bhp at
9 000 rpm
Starting: electric

Transmission: 6-speed chain

Electrics: 12 v electronic
ignition with 16 Ah battery

Frame: Chrome Molybdenum
lattice

Suspension: Upside down
telehydraulic fork with rear
monoshock system

Manufacturer: Ducati Meccanica S.p.A.

Brakes: Twin 320 mm floating
discs and rear 245 mm disc

Tyres: Front is 120/70ZR17
Rear is 180/55ZR17

Dimensions:
Length: 2 030 mm
Width: 780 mm
Wheelbase: 1 430 mm
Clearance: 125 mm
Seat height: 790 mm
Dry weight: 199 kg
Fuel tank: 17 litres

Performance:
Top speed: 240 km/h
Fuel consumption: 5.8 l/100 km

Features: Full fairing.

ENFIELD (India)

Model: 500 Bullet

Engine: 4-str ohv single
Capacity: 499 cc
Bore × Stroke: 84 × 90 mm
Compression ratio: 6.5:1
Carburettor: 28 mm Mikuni
Maximum power: 22 bhp at
5 400 rpm
Starting: kick

Transmission: 4-speed chain

Electrics: 12 v coil ignition with
5.5 Ah battery

Frame: Tubular cradle

Suspension: Telescopic front
fork with twin rear adjustable
shocks

Brakes: 180 mm front drum and
150 mm rear drum

Tyres: Front is 3.25–19
Rear is 3.50–19

Dimensions:
Length: 2 110 mm
Width: 700 mm
Wheelbase: 1 372 mm
Clearance: 140 mm
Seat height: 760 mm
Dry weight: 168 kg
Fuel tank: 14.5 litres

Performance:
Top speed: 130 km/h
Fuel consumption: 3.8 l/100 km

Features: British Royal Enfield
design made in India since 1958.
Optional front disc brake and
electric start. Also as 18 bhp 350
model.

Manufacturer: Enfield India Ltd., 115, Anna Salai, Madras 600 015,
India.

FANTIC (Italy)

Model: Trial K-R00

Engine: 2-str LC reed-valve
single
Capacity: 249.4 cc
Bore × Stroke: 74 × 58 mm
Compression ratio: 10.4:1
Carburettor: 26 mm Dell'Orto
Maximum power: 21 bhp at
5 250 rpm
Starting: Forward moving kick

Transmission: 6-speed chain

Electrics: Flywheel magneto

Frame: Tubular cradle in
Chrome Molybdenum

Suspension: Upside down
telehydraulic fork with alloy rear
Monoshock system

Brakes: 180 mm front disc and
160 mm rear disc

Tyres: Front is 2.75–21
Rear is 4.00–18 tubeless

Dimensions:
Length: 2 000 mm
Width: 830 mm
Wheelbase: 1 310 mm
Clearance: 350 mm
Seat height: 710 mm
Dry weight: 80.5 kg
Fuel tank: 3.5 litres

Performance:
Top speed: 99 km/h
Fuel consumption: 4.3 l/100 km

Features: Light alloy
construction throughout. Unique
refrigeration unit for coolant. Also
in 212 cc version. New in 1991.

Manufacturer: Fabbrica Motoveicoli S.p.A., via Parini, 3, 22061
Barzago (CO), Italy.

FANTIC (Italy)

Model: Trial 307

Engine: 2-str reed-valve single
Capacity: 249.4 cc
Bore × Stroke: 74 × 58 mm
Compression ratio: 10.4:1
Carburettor: 26 mm Dell'Orto
Maximum power: 20.4 bhp at
6 000 rpm
Starting: Forward moving kick

Transmission: 6-speed chain

Electrics: 12 v electronic
ignition/flywheel magneto

Frame: Tubular cradle in
Chrome Molybdenum

Suspension: Upside down
telehydraulic fork with rear
Monoshock system

Brakes: 180 mm front disc and
160 mm rear disc

Tyres: Front is 2.75–21
Rear is 4.00–18

Dimensions:
Length: 2 000 mm
Width: 830 mm
Wheelbase: 1 310 mm
Clearance: 350 mm
Seat height: 700 mm
Dry weight: 79.5 kg
Fuel tank: 3.5 litres

Performance:
Top speed: 99 km/h
Fuel consumption: 4.3 l/100 km

Features: Guard and engine
covers in Magnesium alloy. Low
noise exhaust system. Also in
212 cc and 125 cc versions.

Manufacturer: Fabbrica Motoveicoli S.p.A.

FANTIC (Italy)

Model: Caballero 50 RC

Engine: 2-str LC reed-valve single with Exhaust Power-Valve
Capacity: 49.6 cc
Bore × Stroke: 38.8 × 42 mm
Compression ratio: 13.5:1
Carburettor: 14/12 mm Dell'Orto
Maximum power: 10 bhp at 10 750 rpm
Starting: Forward moving kick

Transmission: 4/6-speed chain

Electrics: 12 v electronic ignition/flywheel magneto

Frame: Duplex tubular cradle

Suspension: Telehydraulic front fork with rear *Monoshock* system

Brakes: 220 mm discs front and rear

Tyres: Front is 3.00–21
Rear is 110/90–18

Dimensions:
Length: 2 180 mm
Width: 830 mm
Wheelbase: 1 400 mm
Clearance: 320 mm
Seat height: 890 mm
Dry weight: 83 kg
Fuel tank: 7.5 litres

Performance:
Top speed: 40/90 km/h
Fuel consumption: 3 l/100 km

Features: Full instrumentation cockpit, thermoplastic tank. In restricted and unrestricted versions.

Manufacturer: Fabbrica Motoveicoli S.p.A.

FANTIC (Italy)

Model: Enduro Oasis 50

Engine: 2-str LC reed-valve
single with Exhaust Power Valve
Capacity: 49.6 cc
Bore × Stroke: 38.8 × 42 mm
Compression ratio: 13.5:1
Carburettor: 14/12 mm Dell'Orto
Maximum power: 8 bhp at
8 000 rpm
Starting: electric/kick

Transmission: 4-speed chain

Electrics: 12 v electronic
ignition with 6 Ah battery

Frame: Duplex tubular cradle

Suspension: Telehydraulic
front fork with rear *Monoshock*
system

Brakes: 220 mm front disc and
rear 118 mm drum

Tyres: Front is 2.75–21
Rear is 4.10–18

Dimensions:
Length: 2 010 mm
Width: 830 mm
Wheelbase: 1 360 mm
Clearance: 320 mm
Seat height: 870 mm
Dry weight: 98 kg
Fuel tank: 20 litres

Performance:
Top speed: 40/85 km/h
Fuel consumption: 2.8 l/100 km

Features: Full instrumentation,
rear parcel rack, twin headlights.
Also in 80 cc version.

Manufacturer: Fabbrica Motoveicoli S.p.A.

FANTIC (Italy)

Model: Joy VK 50

Engine: 2-str reed-valve single
Capacity: 49.5 cc
Bore × Stroke: 40.3 × 38.8 mm
Compression ratio: 8.6:1
Carburettor: 14/12 mm Dell'Orto
Maximum power: 1.5 bhp at
5 500 rpm
Starting: kick

Transmission: Single speed
automatic

Electrics: 12 v flywheel
magneto

Frame: Step-thru

Suspension: Telescopic front
fork with single rear shock
absorber

Brakes: 105 mm drums front
and rear

Tyres: 2.50–16 front and rear

Dimensions:
Length: 1 700 mm
Width: 680 mm
Wheelbase: 1 100 mm
Clearance: 130 mm
Seat height: 780 mm
Dry weight: 50 kg
Fuel tank: 3 litres

Performance:
Top speed: 40 km/h
Fuel consumption: 1.7 l/100 km

Features: Enclosed chain, cast
aluminium wheels. Rear carrier.

Manufacturer: Fabbrica Motoveicoli S.p.A.

GILERA (Italy)

Model: Saturno 500

Engine: 4-str LC dohc 4-valve single
Capacity: 491 cc
Bore × Stroke: 92 × 74 mm
Compression ratio: 9.5:1
Carburettor: 40 mm Dell'Orto
Maximum power: 45 bhp at 7 500 rpm
Starting: electric/kick

Transmission: 5-speed chain

Electrics: 12 v CDI ignition with 14 Ah battery

Frame: Triangulated tubular steel space

Suspension: 40 mm telehydraulic fork with adjustable rear monoshock

Brakes: 300 mm Brembo disc and rear 240 mm disc

Tyres: Front is 110/70VR17
Rear is 140/70VR17

Dimensions:
Length: 2 030 mm
Width: 700 mm
Wheelbase: 1 410 mm
Clearance: ...
Seat height: 790 mm
Dry weight: 140 kg
Fuel tank: 20 litres

Performance:
Top speed: 175 km/h
Fuel consumption: 5 l/100 km

Features: Hand-built machine. Half fairing.

Manufacturer: Gilera Piaggio S.p.A., via C. Battisti, 68, 20043 Arcore (MI), Italy.

GILERA (Italy)

Model: 350 Dakota

Engine: 4-str LC 4-valve single
Capacity: 348.8 cc
Bore × Stroke: 80 × 69.4 mm
Compression ratio: 9.5:1
Carburettor: 2 × 25 mm Dell'Orto
Maximum power: 33 bhp at
7 500 rpm
Starting: kick

Transmission: 5-speed chain

Electrics: 12 v CDI ignition
with 12 Ah battery

Frame: Steel double cradle

Suspension: Air-assisted front
fork with adjustable rear
monoshock

Manufacturer: Gilera-Piaggio S.p.A..

Brakes: 260 mm front disc and
160 mm rear drum

Tyres: Front is 90/90–21
Rear is 4.60–17

Dimensions:
Length: 2 210 mm
Width: 910 mm
Wheelbase: 1 480 mm
Clearance: ...
Seat height: 880 mm
Dry weight: 147 kg
Fuel tank: 13.5 litres

Performance:
Top speed: 145 km/h
Fuel consumption: 5 l/100 km

Features: Electric start option.
Also in 492 cc version.

HARLEY-DAVIDSON (USA)

Model: FLHTC Electra Glide
Ultra Classic

Engine: 4-str ohv Evolution 45°
vee-twin
Capacity: 1 340 cc
Bore × Stroke: 88.8 × 108 mm
Compression ratio: 8.5:1
Carburettor: 40 mm Keihin cv
Maximum power: 58 bhp at
5 000 rpm
Starting: electric

Transmission: 5-speed belt
drive

Electrics: 12 v electronic
ignition with 20 Ah battery

Frame: Steel box section
backbone with twin downtubes

Suspension: Air-assisted front
fork with anti-dive and adjustable
rear shocks

Brakes: 292 mm triple disc
system

Tyres: MT90-16T front and rear

Dimensions:
Length: 2 390 mm
Width: ...
Wheelbase: 1 598 mm
Clearance: 130 mm
Seat height: 711 mm
Dry weight: 347 kg
Fuel tank: 18.9 litres

Performance:
Top speed: 165 km/h
Fuel consumption: 5.6 l/100 km

Features: The full dress tourer,
frame-mounted fairing with
voice-activated CB/intercom and
80-watt stereo system, cruise
control.

Manufacturer: Harley-Davidson Inc., 3700 W. Juneau Ave., Box 653,
Milwaukee, WI 53201, USA.

HARLEY-DAVIDSON (USA)

Model: FLTC Tour Glide Classic

Engine: 4-str ohv Evolution 45° vee-twin
Capacity: 1 340 cc
Bore × Stroke: 88.8 × 108 mm
Compression ratio: 8.5:1
Carburettor: 40 mm Keihin cv
Maximum power: 58 bhp at 5 000 rpm
Starting: electric

Transmission: 5-speed belt drive

Electrics: 12 v electronic ignition with 20 Ah battery

Frame: Steel box section with twin downtubes

Suspension: Telescopic front fork with anti-dive and air-adjustable rear shocks

Manufacturer: Harley-Davidson Inc.

Brakes: 292 mm triple disc system

Tyres: MT90–16T front and rear

Dimensions:
Length: 2 390 mm
Width: ...
Wheelbase: 1 598 mm
Clearance: 130 mm
Seat height: 752 mm
Dry weight: 336 kg
Fuel tank: 18.9 litres

Performance:
Top speed: 195 km/h
Fuel consumption: 6 l/100 km

Features: Tour pack includes 40-watt stereo system, soft look seats and passenger footboards. Frame-mounted fairing.

HARLEY-DAVIDSON (USA)

Model: FXR Super Glide

Engine: 4-str ohv Evolution 45°
vee-twin
Capacity: 1 340 cc
Bore × Stroke: 88.8 × 108 mm
Compression ratio: 8.5:1
Carburettor: 40 mm Keihin cv
Maximum power: 58 bhp at
5 000 rpm
Starting: electric

Transmission: 5-speed belt
drive

Electrics: 12 v electronic
ignition with 19 Ah battery

Frame: Steel box section
backbone with twin downtubes

Suspension: Air-adjustable
front fork with anti-dive and
adjustable rear shocks

Manufacturer: Harley-Davidson Inc.

Brakes: 292 mm discs front and
rear

Tyres: Front is 100/90–19
Rear is 130/90–16

Dimensions:
Length: 2 327 mm
Width: ...
Wheelbase: 1 603 mm
Clearance: 133 mm
Seat height: 660 mm
Dry weight: 261 kg
Fuel tank: 15.9 litres

Performance:
Top speed: 200 km/h
Fuel consumption: 6 l/100km

Features: Centre-fill tank,
buckhorn handlebars and a
stepped seat. Also as a sport
version.

HARLEY-DAVIDSON (USA)

Model: FLSTC Heritage Softail Classic

Engine: 4-str ohv Evolution 45° vee-twin
Capacity: 1 340 cc
Bore × Stroke: 88.8 × 108 mm
Compression ratio: 8.5:1
Carburettor: 40 mm Keihin cv
Maximum power: 58 bhp at 5 000 rpm
Starting: electric

Transmission: 5-speed belt drive

Electrics: 12 v electronic ignition with 19 Ah battery

Frame: Duplex tubular cradle

Suspension: Air-assisted front fork and twin adjustable rear gas shocks

Manufacturer: Harley-Davidson Inc.

Brakes: 292 mm discs front and rear

Tyres: MT90–16T front and rear

Dimensions:
Length: 2 383 mm
Width: ...
Wheelbase: 1 588 mm
Clearance: 133 mm
Seat height: 673 mm
Dry weight: 322 kg
Fuel tank: 15.9 litres

Performance:
Top speed: 180 km/h
Fuel consumption: 6 l/100 km

Features: 1950s style leather saddlebags with king-size windscreen, heel-toe shift lever and chrome passing lights.

HARLEY-DAVIDSON (USA)

Model: FLSTF Fat Boy

Engine: 4-str ohv Evolution 45°
vee-twin
Capacity: 1 340 cc
Bore × Stroke: 88.8 × 108 mm
Compression ratio: 8.5:1
Carburettor: 40 mm Keihin cv
Maximum power: 58 bhp at
5 000 rpm
Starting: electric

Transmission: 5-speed belt
drive

Electrics: 12 v electronic
ignition with 19 Ah battery

Frame: Duplex tubular cradle

Suspension: Air-assisted front
fork with anti-dive and twin
adjustable rear shocks

Manufacturer: Harley-Davidson Inc.

Brakes: 292 mm discs front and
rear

Tyres: MT90–16T front and rear

Dimensions:
Length: 2 380 mm
Width: ...
Wheelbase: 1 588 mm
Clearance: 133 mm
Seat height: 673 mm
Dry weight: 295 kg
Fuel tank: 15.9 litres

Performance:
Top speed: 185 km/h
Fuel consumption: 6 l/100 km

Features: Spun aluminium hub
covers, leather instrument trim,
chrome 'horseshoe' oil tank.

HARLEY-DAVIDSON (USA)

Model: FXDB Sturgis

Engine: 4-str ohv Evolution 45°
vee-twin
Capacity: 1 340 cc
Bore × Stroke: 88.8 × 108 mm
Compression ratio: 8.5:1
Carburettor: 40 mm Keihin cv
Maximum power: 58 bhp at
5 000 rpm
Starting: electric

Transmission: 5-speed belt
drive

Electrics: 12 v electronic
ignition with 19 Ah battery

Frame: Steel box section Dyna
Glide chassis with twin
downtubes

Suspension: Air-assisted front
fork with twin adjustable rear
shocks

Manufacturer: Harley-Davidson Inc.

Brakes: 292 mm discs front and
rear

Tyres: Front is 100/90–19
Rear is 130/90–16

Dimensions:
Length: 2 388 mm
Width: ...
Wheelbase: 1 664 mm
Clearance: 142 mm
Seat height: 675 mm
Dry weight: 271 kg
Fuel tank: 18.9 litres

Performance:
Top speed: 200 km/h
Fuel consumption: 6 l/100 km

Features: CAD-designed frame.
Gloss black engine trim. Named
after a Harley gathering town in
USA.

HARLEY-DAVIDSON (USA)

Model: FXSTS Springer Softail

Engine: 4-str ohv Evolution 45°
vee-twin
Capacity: 1 340 cc
Bore × Stroke: 88 × 108 mm
Compression ratio: 8.5:1
Carburettor: 40 mm Keihin cv
Maximum power: 58 bhp at
5 000 rpm
Starting: electric

Transmission: 5-speed belt
drive

Electrics: 12 v electronic
ignition with 19 Ah battery

Frame: Duplex tubular cradle

Suspension: Air-assisted front
fork with anti-dive and air-
adjustable rear shocks

Manufacturer: Harley-Davidson Inc.

Brakes: 292 mm discs front and
rear

Tyres: Front is MH90–21
Rear is 130/90B16

Dimensions:
Length: 2 350 mm
Width: ...
Wheelbase: 1 638 mm
Clearance: 137 mm
Seat height: 663 mm
Dry weight: 283 kg
Fuel tank: 18.5 litres

Performance:
Top speed: 195 km/h
Fuel consumption: 6 l/100 km

Features: Brake and gear lever
forward foot controls, 1948 model
Springer front end.

HARLEY-DAVIDSON (USA)

Model: FXRS-SP Low Rider Sport

Engine: 4-str ohv Evolution 45° vee-twin
Capacity: 1 340 cc
Bore × Stroke: 88.8 × 108 mm
Compression ratio: 8.5:1
Carburettor: 40 mm Keihin cv
Maximum power: 58 bhp at 5 000 rpm
Starting: electric

Transmission: 5-speed belt drive

Electrics: 12 v electronic ignition with 19 Ah battery

Frame: Steel box section backbone with twin downtubes

Suspension: Telescopic front fork with anti-dive and adjustable rear shocks

Manufacturer: Harley-Davidson Inc.

Brakes: 292 mm triple disc system

Tyres: Front is 100/90–19
Rear is 130/90–16

Dimensions:
Length: 2 370 mm
Width: ...
Wheelbase: 1 643 mm
Clearance: 152 mm
Seat height: 698 mm
Dry weight: 265 kg
Fuel tank: 15.9 litres

Performance:
Top speed: 200 km/h
Fuel consumption: 6 l/100 km

Features: Low handlebar and large saddle-style seat. Sport-style front fender.

HARLEY-DAVIDSON (USA)

Model: XLH Sportster 883

Engine: 4-str ohv Evolution 45°
vee-twin
Capacity: 883 cc
Bore × Stroke: 76.2 × 96.8 mm
Compression ratio: 9:1
Carburettor: 40 mm Keihin cv
Maximum power: 49 bhp at
6 000 rpm
Starting: electric

Transmission: 5-speed chain

Electrics: 12 v electronic
ignition with 19 Ah battery

Frame: Duplex tubular cradle

Suspension: Telescopic front
fork with twin long travel rear
shocks

Manufacturer: Harley-Davidson Inc.

Brakes: 292 mm discs front and
rear

Tyres: Front is 100/90–19
Rear is 130/90–19

Dimensions:
Length: 2 222 mm
Width: ...
Wheelbase: 1 520 mm
Clearance: 170 mm
Seat height: 720 mm
Dry weight: 214 kg
Fuel tank: 8.5 litres

Performance:
Top speed: 185 km/h
Fuel consumption: 5.2 l/100 km

Features: Also in Deluxe and
Hugger versions. No frills Harley
with single seat.

HERCULES (Germany)

Model: KX 5 50

Engine: 2-str single
Capacity: 49 cc
Bore × Stroke: 38 × 44 mm
Compression ratio: 11.5:1
Carburettor: 19 mm Bing
Maximum power: 4 bhp at
5 000 rpm
Starting: kick

Transmission: 5-speed chain

Electrics: 12 v Motoplat
ignition

Frame: Single tubular cradle

Suspension: Telescopic front
fork with twin rear hydraulic
shocks

Brakes: 220 mm front disc and
140 mm rear drum

Tyres: 2.75–17 front and rear

Dimensions:
Length: 1 930 mm
Width: 720 mm
Wheelbase: 1 200 m
Clearance: 160 mm
Seat height: 795 mm
Dry weight: 98 kg
Fuel tank: 14 litres

Performance:
Top speed: 50 km/h
Fuel consumption: 2.3 l/100 km

Features: Handlebar fairing and
rear carrier.

Manufacturer: Hercules GmbH., 8500 Nürnberg 70, Germany.

HESKETH (United Kingdom)

Model: V1000

Engine: 4-str dohc 4-valve 90°
vee-twin
Capacity: 992.3 cc
Bore × Stroke: 95 × 70 mm
Compression ratio: 10.5:1
Carburettor: 2 × 36 mm Dell'Orto
Maximum power: 80 bhp at
6 200 rpm
Starting: electric

Transmission: 5-speed chain

Electrics: 12 v electronic
ignition with 27 Ah battery

Frame: Duplex tubular cradle

Suspension: Telehydraulic
front fork with twin adjustable
rear shocks

Brakes: 280 mm triple floating
disc system

Tyres: Front is 100/90V19
Rear is 130/90V17

Dimensions:
Length: 2 235 mm
Width: 712 mm
Wheelbase: 1 510 mm
Clearance: 140 mm
Seat height: 838 mm
Dry weight: 247 kg
Fuel tank: 23 litres

Performance:
Top speed: 210 km/h
Fuel consumption: 6 l/100 km

Features: Vampire model has
full fairing. Made to order
machines.

Manufacturer: Mick Broom Engineering, North Wing, Easton Neston,
Towcester, Northants, NN12 7HS, England.

HONDA (Japan)

Model: GL1500 Gold Wing

Engine: 4-str LC sohc opposed
flat six
Capacity: 1 520 cc
Bore × Stroke: 71 × 64 mm
Compression ratio: 9.8:1
Carburettor: 2 × 36 mm Keihin cv
Maximum power: 92 bhp at
5 000 rpm
Starting: electric

Transmission: 5-speed shaft
drive and reverse

Electrics: 12 v electronic
ignition with 20 Ah battery

Frame: Duplex tubular cradle

Suspension: Air-assisted
telescopic fork with rear
monoshock system

Brakes: Twin 296 mm discs and
rear 316 mm disc

Tyres: Front is 130/70–18
Rear is 160/80–16

Dimensions:
Length: 2 630 mm
Width: 955 mm
Wheelbase: 1 700 mm
Clearance: 146 mm
Seat height: 770 mm
Dry weight: 367 kg
Fuel tank: 24 litres

Performance:
Top speed: 200 km/h
Fuel consumption: 6 l/100 km

Features: 10th anniversary
model. Air management system,
updated audio system, optional
adjustable foot boards.

Manufacturer: Honda Motor Co. Ltd., 1–1–2 Chome, Minami-Aoyama
Minato-ku, Tokyo 107, Japan.

HONDA (Japan)

Model: Pan European ST1100

Engine: 4-str LC dohc 4-valve
90° vee-four
Capacity: 1 084 cc
Bore × Stroke: 73 × 64.8 mm
Compression ratio: 10.3:1
Carburettor: 4 × 34 mm VD
Keihin
Maximum power: 100 bhp at
7 500 rpm
Starting: electric

Transmission: 5-speed shaft
drive

Electrics: 12 v electronic
ignition with 12 Ah battery

Frame: Steel double cradle

Suspension: Telescopic fork
with TRAC anti-dive and rear
adjustable monoshock

Manufacturer: Honda Motor Co. Ltd.

Brakes: 316 mm triple disc
system

Tyres: Front is 110/80V18
Rear is 160/70V17

Dimensions:
Length: 2 285 mm
Width: 780 mm
Wheelbase: 1 555 mm
Clearance: 145 mm
Seat height: 800 mm
Dry weight: 283 kg
Fuel tank: 28 litres

Performance:
Top speed: 200 km/h
Fuel consumption: 5.8 l/100 km

Features: Aerodynamic full
fairing, designed for the European
market, 35-litre panniers, twin
headlights. Torque Reactive Anti-
dive Control.

HONDA (Japan)

Model: CBR1000F

Engine: 4-str LC dohc 4-valve
in-line four
Capacity: 998 cc
Bore × Stroke: 77 × 53.6 mm
Compression ratio: 10.5:1
Carburettor: 4 × 38 mm Keihin cv
Maximum power: 132 bhp at
9 500 rpm
Starting: electric

Transmission: 6-speed chain

Electrics: 12 v digital ignition
with 9 Ah battery

Frame: Steel box section
diamond

Suspension: Air-assisted fork
with TRAC anti-dive and
adjustable rear *Pro-Link*

Manufacturer: Honda Motor Co Ltd.

Brakes: 296 mm twin discs and
rear 276 mm disc

Tyres: Front is 120/70V17
Rear is 170/60V17

Dimensions:
Length: 2 225 mm
Width: 780 mm
Wheelbase: 1 505 mm
Clearance: 135 mm
Seat height: 780 mm
Dry weight: 230 kg
Fuel tank: 21 litres

Performance:
Top speed: 260 km/h
Fuel consumption: 7.6 l/100 km

Features: Fully enclosed
bodywork with ram-air ducts for
rider comfort.

HONDA (Japan)

Model: RC30

Engine: 4-str LC dohc 4-valve
90° vee-four
Capacity: 748 cc
Bore × Stroke: 70 × 48.6 mm
Compression ratio: 11:1
Carburettor: 4 × 34 mm Keihin cv
Maximum power: 112 bhp at
11 000 rpm
Starting: electric

Transmission: 6-speed chain

Electrics: 12 v electronic
ignition

Frame: Aluminium box section

Suspension: Air-assisted front
fork with *Pro-Arm* monoshock
system

Brakes: Twin 310 mm front
discs and 220 mm rear disc

Tyres: Front is 120/70V17
Rear is 170/60V18

Dimensions:
Length: 2 085 mm
Width: 700 mm
Wheelbase: 1 405 mm
Clearance: 130 mm
Seat height: 785 mm
Dry weight: 185 kg
Fuel tank: 18 litres

Performance:
Top speed: 250 km/h
Fuel consumption: 7 l/100 km

Features: Full fairing with twin
headlights. Race pack options
boosts output to 130 bhp.

Manufacturer: Honda Motor Co. Ltd.

HONDA (Japan)

Model: VFR750F

Engine: 4-str LC dohc 4-valve
90° vee-four
Capacity: 748 cc
Bore × Stroke: 70 × 48.6 mm
Compression ratio: 11:1
Carburettor: 4 × 34 mm Keihin cv
Maximum power: 100 bhp at
10 500 rpm
Starting: electric

Transmission: 6-speed chain

Electrics: 12 v electronic
ignition with 12 Ah battery

Frame: Aluminium box section

Suspension: Air-assisted front
fork with *Pro-Arm* monoshock
system.

Brakes: Twin 296 mm front
discs and rear 256 mm disc

Tyres: Front is 120/70VR17
Rear is 170/60VR17

Dimensions:
Length: 2 180 mm
Width: 700 mm
Wheelbase: 1 470 mm
Clearance: 130 mm
Seat height: 800 mm
Dry weight: 216 kg
Fuel tank: 20 litres

Performance:
Top speed: 220 km/h
Fuel consumption: 6.4 l/100 km

Features: Super Sports model,
ram-air screen and twin
headlights. TRAC anti-dive
system.

Manufacturer: Honda Motor Co Ltd.

HONDA (Japan)

Model: XRV750 Africa Twin

Engine: 4-str LC sohc 52°
3-valve vee-twin
Capacity: 742 cc
Bore × Stroke: 81 × 72 mm
Compression ratio: 9:1
Carburettor: 2 × 34 mm Keihin
Maximum power: 61.4 bhp at
7 500 rpm
Starting: electric

Transmission: 5-speed chain

Electrics: 12 v electronic
ignition with 12 Ah battery

Frame: Steel box section cradle

Suspension: Telescopic front
fork with rear *Pro-Link*
monoshock system.

Brakes: Twin 276 mm front
discs and rear 256 mm disc

Tyres: Front is 90/90–21
Rear is 130/90–17

Dimensions:
Length: 2 330 mm
Width: 900 mm
Wheelbase: 1 560 mm
Clearance: 255 mm
Seat height: 890 mm
Dry weight: 210 kg
Fuel tank: 24 litres

Performance:
Top speed: 180 km/h
Fuel consumption: 6.6 l/100 km

Features: Based on Paris-Dakar
NXR race winner. Twin headlight
fairing and engine bashplate.

Manufacturer: Honda Motor Co. Ltd.

HONDA (Japan)

Model: NX650 Dominator

Engine: 4-str sohc 4-valve single
Capacity: 644 cc
Bore × Stroke: 100 × 82 mm
Compression ratio: 8.3:1
Carburettor: 40 mm Keihin
Maximum power: 45 bhp at 6 000 rpm
Starting: electric/kick

Transmission: 5-speed chain

Electrics: 12 v electronic ignition

Frame: box section cradle

Suspension: Telescopic front fork with *Pro-Link* monoshock system

Brakes: 256 mm front disc and rear 220 mm disc

Tyres: Front is 90/90–21
Rear is 120/90–17

Dimensions:
Length: 2 190 mm
Width: 890 mm
Wheelbase: 1 435 mm
Clearance: 245 mm
Seat height: 865 mm
Dry weight: 152 kg
Fuel tank: 13 litres

Performance:
Top speed: 190 km/h
Fuel consumption: 5.6 l/100 km

Features: Automatic decompressor for starting. Top fairing, enclosed front disc, dual exhaust system.

Manufacturer: Honda Motor Co. Ltd.

HONDA (Japan)

Model: CBR600F

Engine: 4-str LC dohc 4-valve
in-line four
Capacity: 599 cc
Bore × Stroke: 65 × 45.2 mm
Compression ratio: 11.6:1
Carburettor: 4 × 34 mm Keihin cv
Maximum power: 100 bhp at
12 000 rpm
Starting: electric

Transmission: 6-speed chain

Electrics: 12 v digital ignition
with 12 Ah battery

Frame: Twin spar steel diamond

Suspension: Adjustable
telescopic front fork with
adjustable *Pro-Link* monoshock

Brakes: Twin 276 mm front
discs and 220 mm rear disc

Tyres: Front is 120/60ZR17
Rear is 160/60ZR17 radials

Dimensions:
Length: 2 130 mm
Width: 695 mm
Wheelbase: 1 405 mm
Clearance: 140 mm
Seat height: 810 mm
Dry weight: 185 kg
Fuel tank: 16 litres

Performance:
Top speed: 245 km/h
Fuel consumption: 6.4 l/100 km

Features: 4–2–1 stainless steel
exhaust, fully-enclosed fairing,
computer-designed lightweight
chassis.

Manufacturer: Honda Motor Co. Ltd.

HONDA (Japan)

Model: NTV600 Revere

Engine: 4-str LC sohc 3-valve
52° vee-twin
Capacity: 583 cc
Bore × Stroke: 75 × 66 mm
Compression ratio: 9.2:1
Carburettor: 2 × 34 mm Keihin
Maximum power: 55 bhp at
8 000 rpm
Starting: electric

Transmission: 5-speed shaft
drive

Electrics: 12 v electronic
ignition with 12 Ah battery

Frame: Box section diamond

Suspension: Telescopic front
fork with rear single sided
swinging arm

Manufacturer: Honda Motor Co. Ltd.

Brakes: 310 mm front disc and
273 mm rear disc

Tyres: Front is 110/80–17
Rear is 150/70–17

Dimensions:
Length: 2 145 mm
Width: 710 mm
Wheelbase: 1 460 mm
Clearance: 150 mm
Seat height: 780 mm
Dry weight: 188 kg
Fuel tank: 17 litres

Performance:
Top speed: 175 km/h
Fuel consumption: 5 l/100 km

Features: Cast wheels, optional
panniers.

HONDA (Japan)

Model: Transalp 600V

Engine: 4-str LC sohc 52° 3-valve vee-twin
Capacity: 583 cc
Bore × Stroke: 75 × 66 mm
Compression ratio: 9.2:1
Carburettor: 2 × 32 mm Keihin VD
Maximum power: 55 bhp at 8 000 rpm
Starting: electric

Transmission: 5-speed chain

Electrics: 12 v CDI ignition with 12 Ah battery

Frame: Lightweight box section cradle

Suspension: Leading axle front fork with rear adjustable *Pro-Link* system

Brakes: 276 mm front disc and rear 130 mm drum

Tyres: Front is 90/90–21
Rear is 130/80–17

Dimensions:
Length: 2 265 mm
Width: 865 mm
Wheelbase: 1 505 mm
Clearance: 225 mm
Seat height: 850 mm
Dry weight: 175 kg
Fuel tank: 18 litres

Performance:
Top speed: 170 km/h
Fuel consumption: 6.2 l/100 km

Features: Dual purpose touring bike. Frame-mounted fairing, engine bash plate and rear carrier.

Manufacturer: Honda Motor Co. Ltd.

HONDA (Japan)

Model: VFR400R3

Engine: 4-str LC dohc 4-valve
90° vee-four
Capacity: 399 cc
Bore × Stroke: 55 × 42 mm
Compression ratio: 11.3:1
Carburettor: 4 × 34 mm Keihin
Maximum power: 63 bhp at
12 500 rpm
Starting: electric

Transmission: 6-speed chain

Electrics: 12 v digital ignition

Frame: Ladder shaped
aluminium twin-tube

Suspension: Air-assisted front
fork with adjustable *Pro-arm*
monoshock

Manufacturer: Honda Motor Co. Ltd.

Brakes: Twin 296 mm discs and
rear 220 mm disc

Tyres: Front is 120/60R17
Rear is 150/60R18

Dimensions:
Length: 1 985 mm
Width: 705 mm
Wheelbase: 1 345 mm
Clearance: 125 mm
Seat height: 775 mm
Dry weight: 170 kg
Fuel tank: 18 litres

Performance:
Top speed: 210 km/h
Fuel consumption: 6 l/100 km

Features: Baby version of the
RC30. Dual radiator, twin
headlights.

HONDA (Japan)

Model: CN250

Engine: 4-str LC sohc single
Capacity: 244 cc
Bore × Stroke: 72 × 60 mm
Compression ratio: 10:1
Carburettor: 30 mm Mikuni
Maximum power: 17 bhp at
7 500 rpm
Starting: electric

Transmission: Honda V-Matic
automatic

Electrics: 12 v CDI ignition

Frame: Monocoque

Suspension: Trailing link fork
with twin hydraulic rear shocks

Brakes: 220 mm front disc and
130 mm rear drum

Tyres: Front is 4.00–12
Rear is 120/90–10

Dimensions:
Length: 2 265 mm
Width: 745 mm
Wheelbase: 1 625 mm
Clearance: 130 mm
Seat height: 665 mm
Dry weight: 156 kg
Fuel tank: 12 litres

Performance:
Top speed: 120 km/h
Fuel consumption: 3.5 l/100 km

Features: Feet-forward
commuter scooter, split level dual
seat, boot style storage for two
helmets, liquid crystal display
instrumentation.

Manufacturer: Honda Motor Co. Ltd.

HONDA (Japan)

Model: NSR125R

Engine: 2-str LC single
Capacity: 124.8 cc
Bore × Stroke: 54 × 54.5 mm
Compression ratio: 7.2:1
Carburettor: 24 mm Dell'Orto
Maximum power: 12 bhp at
7 500 rpm
Starting: electric

Transmission: 6-speed chain

Electrics: 12 v CDI ignition

Frame: Aluminium cast
diamond

Suspension: Marzocchi front
fork with rear *Pro-Link*
monoshock system.

Brakes: 316 mm front disc and
220 mm rear disc

Tyres: Front is 100/80—17
Rear is 130/70—18

Dimensions:
Length: 2 015 mm
Width: 690 mm
Wheelbase: 1 350 mm
Clearance: 160 mm
Seat height: 780 mm
Dry weight: 127 kg
Fuel tank: 12 litres

Performance:
Top speed: 117 km/h
Fuel consumption: 4 l/100 km

Features: Sports learner with
race-replica styling. Produced by
Honda in Italy. Cast wheels and
removable rear seat squab.

Manufacturer: Honda Motor Co. Ltd.

HONDA (Japan)

Model: CG125

Engine: 4-str ohv single
Capacity: 124 cc
Bore × Stroke: 56.5 × 49.5 mm
Compression ratio: 9.2:1
Carburettor: 24 mm Keihin
Maximum power: 11 bhp at
9 000 rpm
Starting: kick

Transmission: 5-speed chain

Electrics: 12 v coil ignition

Frame: Tubular cradle

Suspension: Telescopic front
fork with twin hydraulic rear
shocks

Brakes: Drums front and rear

Tyres: Front is 2.50–18
Rear is 3.00–17

Dimensions:
Length: 1 935 mm
Width: 745 mm
Wheelbase: 1 280 mm
Clearance: 150 mm
Seat height: 755 mm
Dry weight: 99 kg
Fuel tank: 12 litres

Performance:
Top speed: 105 km/h
Fuel consumption: 2 l/100 km

Features: Fuel economy model.
Fully-enclosed chain.

Manufacturer: Honda Motor Co. Ltd.

HONDA (Japan)

Model: MTX125R

Engine: 2-str LC single
Capacity: 124 cc
Bore × Stroke: 56 × 50.6 mm
Compression ratio: 7.5:1
Carburettor: 24 mm Dell'Orto
Maximum power: 12 bhp at
7 500 rpm
Starting: kick

Transmission: 6-speed chain

Electrics: 12 v CDI ignition

Frame: Steel tubular cradle

Suspension: Air-assisted
leading link fork with rear
adjustable *Pro-Link*

Brakes: 240 mm front disc and
rear drum

Tyres: Front is 2.75–21
Rear is 4.10–18

Dimensions:
Length: 2 090 mm
Width: 830 mm
Wheelbase: 1 345 mm
Clearance: 285 mm
Seat height: 845 mm
Dry weight: 99 kg
Fuel tank: 9 litres

Performance:
Top speed: 112 km/h
Fuel consumption: 3 l/100 km

Features: Trail model with rear
carrier.

Manufacturer: Honda Motor Co. Ltd.

HONDA (Japan)

Model: H100S

Engine: 2-str single
Capacity: 99 cc
Bore × Stroke: 50.5 × 49.5 mm
Compression ratio: 7.2 : 1
Carburettor: 18 mm Keihin
Maximum power: 11 bhp at
6 000 rpm
Starting: kick

Transmission: 5-speed chain

Electrics: 6 v flywheel magneto
ignition

Frame: Beam type

Suspension: Telescopic front
fork with twin hydraulic rear
shocks

Manufacturer: Honda Motor Co. Ltd.

Brakes: Drums front and rear

Tyres: Front is 2.50–18
Rear is 2.75–18

Dimensions:
Length: 1 860 mm
Width: 690 mm
Wheelbase: 1 200 mm
Clearance: 160 mm
Seat height: 770 mm
Dry weight: 86 kg
Fuel tank: 11 litres

Performance:
Top speed: 105 km/h
Fuel consumption: 3 l/100 km

Features: Lightweight
commuter model.

HONDA (Japan)

Model: C90G Cub

Engine: 4-str sohc single
Capacity: 85 cc
Bore × Stroke: 47 × 49.5 mm
Compression ratio: 8.8:1
Carburettor: 16 mm Keihin
Maximum power: 7.5 bhp at
5 500 rpm
Starting: kick

Transmission: 3-speed
automatic

Electrics: 12 v CDI ignition
with 5 Ah battery

Frame: Step-thru pressed steel

Suspension: Bottom link front
fork with twin rear shocks

Manufacturer: Honda Motor Co. Ltd.

Brakes: Drums front and rear

Tyres: 2.50–17 front and rear

Dimensions:
Length: 1 835 mm
Width: 660 mm
Wheelbase: 1 175 mm
Clearance: 130 mm
Seat height: 765 mm
Dry weight: 82 kg
Fuel tank: 3.5 litres

Performance:
Top speed: 80 km/h
Fuel consumption: 2 l/100 km

Features: Legshields, fully-
enclosed chain. Also available
with electric start.

HONDA (Japan)

Model: NH80 Vision

Engine: 2-str single
Capacity: 79 cc
Bore × Stroke: 48 × 44 mm
Compression ratio: 7:1
Carburettor: 16 mm Keihin
Maximum power: 6.6 bhp at
6 500 rpm
Starting: electric

Transmission: Honda V-Matic
automatic

Electrics: 12 v CDI ignition

Frame: Monocoque

Suspension: Leading link front
fork with rear single shocker

Manufacturer: Honda Motor Co. Ltd.

Brakes: Drums front and rear

Tyres: 3.50–10 front and rear

Dimensions:
Length: 1 675 mm
Width: 665 mm
Wheelbase: 1 170 mm
Clearance: 110 mm
Seat height: 710 mm
Dry weight: 74 kg
Fuel tank: 5.3 litres

Performance:
Top speed: 75 km/h
Fuel consumption: 3.5 l/100 km

Features: City runabout. Rear
carrier.

HONDA (Japan)

Model: SA50 Vision Met-in

Engine: 2-str single
Capacity: 49 cc
Bore × Stroke: 41 × 37.4 mm
Compression ratio: 6.5:1
Carburettor: 14 mm Keihin
Maximum power: 4 bhp at
6 000 rpm
Starting: electric/kick

Transmission: Honda V-Matic
automatic

Electrics: 12 v CDI ignition

Frame: Monocoque

Suspension: Trailing bottom
link fork with single rear shocker

Manufacturer: Honda Motor Co. Ltd.

Brakes: Drums front and rear

Tyres: 2.75–10 front and rear

Dimensions:
Length: 1 710 mm
Width: 650 mm
Wheelbase: 1 200 mm
Clearance: 100 mm
Seat height: 750 mm
Dry weight: 65 kg
Fuel tank: 5 litres

Performance:
Top speed: 56 km/h
Fuel consumption: 1.5 l/100 km

Features: Safety helmet
storage space, rear carrier.

HONDA (Japan)

Model: SH50 City Express

Engine: 2-str single
Capacity: 49.4 cc
Bore × Stroke: 44 × 39.3 mm
Compression ratio: 7:1
Carburettor: 12 mm Keihin
Maximum power: 3.1 bhp at
5 500 rpm
Starting: electric

Transmission: Honda V-Matic
automatic

Electrics: 12 v CDI ignition

Frame: Step-thru flat floor
design

Suspension: Telescopic front
fork with twin hydraulic rear
shocks

Manufacturer: Honda Motor Co. Ltd.

Brakes: Drums front and rear

Tyres: Front is 2.50–16
Rear is 2.75–16

Dimensions:
Length: 1 800 mm
Width: 694 mm
Wheelbase: 1 210 mm
Clearance: 140 mm
Seat height: 750 mm
Dry weight: 68 kg
Fuel tank: 4.5 litres

Performance:
Top speed: 50 km/h
Fuel consumption: 1.5 l/100 km

Features: Leg shields, rear
carrier.

HONDA (Japan)

Model: MT50S

Engine: 2-str single
Capacity: 49 cc
Bore × Stroke: 39 × 41.4 mm
Compression ratio: 7.6:1
Carburettor: 12 mm Keihin
Maximum power: 2.6 bhp at
6 500 rpm
Starting: kick

Transmission: 5-speed chain

Electrics: 12 v CDI ignition

Frame: Moto cross style

Suspension: Telescopic front
fork with twin hydraulic rear
shocks

Manufacturer: Honda Motor Co. Ltd.

Brakes: Drums front and rear

Tyres: Front is 2.50–19
Rear is 3.00–16

Dimensions:
Length: 1 905 mm
Width: 780 mm
Wheelbase: 1 240 mm
Clearance: 220 mm
Seat height: 790 mm
Dry weight: 81 kg
Fuel tank: 6.8 litres

Performance:
Top speed: 55 km/h
Fuel consumption: 2 l/100 km

Features: Automatic oil
injection system.

HONDA (Japan)

Model: PA50 Camino

Engine: 2-str single
Capacity: 49 cc
Bore × Stroke: 40 × 39.6 mm
Compression ratio: 6.7:1
Carburettor: 12 mm Keihin
Maximum power: 2.3 bhp at
5 500 rpm
Starting: pedal

Transmission: Honda V-Matic
automatic

Electrics: 6 v flywheel magneto
ignition

Frame: Pressed steel spine

Suspension: Telescopic front
fork with twin rear shocks

Manufacturer: Honda Motor Co. Ltd.

Brakes: Drums front and rear

Tyres: 2.00–17 front and rear

Dimensions:
Length: 1 650 mm
Width: 620 mm
Wheelbase: 1 055 mm
Clearance: 120 mm
Seat height: 775 mm
Dry weight: 46.5 kg
Fuel tank: 3 litres

Performance:
Top speed: 48 km/h
Fuel consumption: 1.2 l/100 km

Features: Fully-enclosed
transmission. Adjustable seat
height, rear carrier. Built in
Belgium.

HUSQVARNA (Sweden)

Model: 610 TE

Engine: 4-str LC sohc 4-valve single
Capacity: 577 cc
Bore × Stroke: 98 × 76.5 mm
Compression ratio: 10.2:1
Carburettor: 40 mm Dell'Orto
Maximum power: ...
Starting: kick

Transmission: 6-speed chain

Electrics: 12 v CDI ignition

Frame: Single tubular cradle

Suspension: Upside down telehydraulic fork with rear *Soft-Damp* monoshock

Brakes: 240 mm Brembo disc and rear 220 mm disc

Tyres: Front is 90/90–21
Rear is 140/80–18

Dimensions:
Length: 2 200 mm
Width: 830 mm
Wheelbase: 1 500 mm
Clearance: 340 mm
Seat height: 945 mm
Dry weight: 116 kg
Fuel tank: 9 litres

Performance:
Top speed: ...
Fuel consumption: ...

Features: European Champion and frequent Six Days Event winner in the 1980s.

Manufacturer: Husqvarna Motorcyklar AB., Box 103, 59900 Ödeshög, Sweden.

HUSQVARNA (Sweden)

Model: TE 350

Engine: 4-str LC sohc 4-valve single
Capacity: 349 cc
Bore × Stroke: 84 × 63 mm
Compression ratio: 10.2:1
Carburettor: 34 mm Dell'Orto
Maximum power: ...
Starting: kick

Transmission: 6-speed chain

Electrics: 12 v CDI ignition

Frame: Single tubular cradle

Suspension: Upside down telehydraulic fork and rear *Soft-Damp* monoshock

Brakes: 240 mm front disc and 220 mm rear disc

Tyres: Front is 90/90–21
Rear is 140/80–18

Dimensions:
Length: 2 200 mm
Width: 830 mm
Wheelbase: 1 500 mm
Clearance: 340 mm
Seat height: 945 mm
Dry weight: 116 kg
Fuel tank: 9 litres

Performance:
Top speed: ...
Fuel consumption: ...

Features: 1990 Enduro world champion.

Manufacturer: Husqvarna Motorcyklar AB.

HUSQVARNA (Sweden)

Model: 125 WR

Engine: 2-str LC reed-valve single
Capacity: 124.63 cc
Bore × Stroke: 56 × 50.6 mm
Compression ratio: 8.9:1
Carburettor: 37 mm Dell'Orto
Maximum power: ...
Starting: kick

Transmission: 6-speed chain

Electrics: 12 v CDI ignition

Frame: Single tubular cradle

Suspension: Upside down telehydraulic fork with rear *Soft-Damp* monoshock

Brakes: 240 mm floating disc and 220 mm rear disc

Tyres: Front is 90/90–21
Rear is 120/90–18

Dimensions:
Length: 2 195 mm
Width: 830 mm
Wheelbase: 1 490 mm
Clearance: 345 mm
Seat height: 920 mm
Dry weight: 93 kg
Fuel tank: 8.3 litres

Performance:
Top speed: ...
Fuel consumption: ...

Features: Whitepower shock absorbers fitted.

Manufacturer: Husqvarna Motorcyklar AB.

JAWA (Czechoslovakia)

Model: 350 (Type 638)

Engine: 2-str single with aluminium alloy cylinders
Capacity: 343.47 cc
Bore × Stroke: 58 × 65 mm
Compression ratio: 10.2:1
Carburettor: 28 mm Jikov
Maximum power: 25 bhp at 5 500 rpm
Starting: kick

Transmission: 4-speed chain

Electrics: 12 v coil ignition with 5 Ah battery

Frame: Tubular cradle

Suspension: Telescopic front fork with twin adjustable rear shocks

Brakes: 160 mm drums front and rear

Tyres: Front is 3.25–18
Rear is 3.50–18

Dimensions:
Length: 2 110 mm
Width: 750 mm
Wheelbase: 1 350 mm
Clearance: 203 mm
Seat height: 810 mm
Dry weight: 156 kg
Fuel tank: 17 litres

Performance:
Top speed: 125 km/h
Fuel consumption: 4.2 l/100 km

Features: Fully-enclosed chain, tool kit and tyre inflator. The type 632 is a basic, unfaired version. Can be fitted with Velorex sidecar or Tradesman Box.

Manufacturer: Jawa Týnec nad Sázavou, Čzechoslovakia.

KAWASAKI (Japan)

Model: ZZ-R 1100

Engine: 4-str LC dohc 4-valve
in-line four
Capacity: 1 052 cc
Bore × Stroke: 76 × 58 mm
Compression ratio: 11:1
Carburettor: 4 × 40 mm Keihin cv
Maximum power: 125 bhp at
10 000 rpm
Starting: electric

Transmission: 6-speed chain

Electrics: 12 v electronic
ignition

Frame: Aluminium perimeter

Suspension: 43 mm adjustable
front fork with rear adjustable
Uni-Trak system

Brakes: Twin 310 mm floating
discs and rear 250 mm disc

Tyres: Front is 120/70VR17
Rear is 170/60VR17

Dimensions:
Length: 2 165 mm
Width: 720 mm
Wheelbase: 1 480 mm
Clearance: 110 mm
Seat height: 780 mm
Dry weight: 228 kg
Fuel tank: 21 litres

Performance:
Top speed: 240 km/h
Fuel consumption: 6.5 l/100 km

Features: Full fairing. In
unrestricted form delivers around
150 bhp with a top speed of
285 km/h.

Manufacturer: Kawasaki Heavy Industries Ltd., 1–1, Kawasaki-cho,
Akashi, 673, Japan.

KAWASAKI (Japan)

Model: ZX-10

Engine: 4-str LC dohc 4-valve
in-line four
Capacity: 997 cc
Bore × Stroke: 74 × 58 mm
Compression ratio: 11:1
Carburettor: 4 × 36 mm Keihin cv
Maximum power: 125 bhp at
9 500 rpm
Starting: electric

Transmission: 6-speed chain

Electrics: 12 v digital ignition
with 14 Ah battery

Frame: Aluminium 'E-Box'
perimeter

Suspension: 41 mm telescopic
front fork with air-adjustable *Uni-
Trak* system

Brakes: Twin 272 mm front
discs and rear 222 mm disc

Tyres: Front is 120/70VR17
Rear is 160/60VR18

Dimensions:
Length: 2 170 mm
Width: 715 mm
Wheelbase: 1 490 mm
Clearance: 125 mm
Seat height: 790 mm
Dry weight: 222 kg
Fuel tank: 22 litres

Performance:
Top speed: 270 km/h
Fuel consumption: 6 l/100 km

Features: Full fairing, radial
tyres.

Manufacturer: Kawasaki Heavy Industries Ltd.

KAWASAKI (Japan)

Model: 1000 GTR

Engine: 4-str LC dohc 4-valve in-line four
Capacity: 997 cc
Bore × Stroke: 74 × 58 mm
Compression ratio: 10.2:1
Carburettor: 4 × 34 mm Keihin cv
Maximum power: 110 bhp at 9 500 rpm
Starting: electric

Transmission: 6-speed shaft drive

Electrics: 12 v electronic ignition with 18 Ah battery

Frame: Diamond section perimeter

Suspension: Air-adjustable telescopic fork with air-adjustable *Uni-Trak* system

Brakes: Twin 236 mm front discs and rear 246 mm disc

Tyres: Front is 110/80VR18
Rear is 150/80VR16

Dimensions:
Length: 2 290 mm
Width: 930 mm
Wheelbase: 1 555 mm
Clearance: 140 mm
Seat height: 815 mm
Dry weight: 265 kg
Fuel tank: 28.5 litres

Performance:
Top speed: 210 km/h
Fuel consumption: 7 l/100 km

Features: Full fairing, factory-fitted paniers.

Manufacturer: Kawasaki Heavy Industries Ltd.

KAWASAKI (Japan)

Model: GPZ900R

Engine: 4-str LC dohc 4-valve
in-line four
Capacity: 908 cc
Bore × Stroke: 72.5 × 55 mm
Compression ratio: 11:1
Carburettor: 4 × 34 mm Keihin cv
Maximum power: 115 bhp at
9 500 rpm
Starting: electric

Transmission: 6-speed chain

Electrics: 12 v electronic
ignition with 14 Ah battery

Frame: Lightweight diamond
chassis

Suspension: 41 mm telescopic
front fork with rear *Uni-Trak*
system

Brakes: Twin 265 mm front
discs and rear 222 mm disc

Tyres: Front is 120/70V17
Rear is 150/70V18

Dimensions:
Length: 2 200 mm
Width: 730 mm
Wheelbase: 1 500 mm
Clearance: 140 mm
Seat height: 790 mm
Dry weight: 234 kg
Fuel tank: 22 litres

Performance:
Top speed: 248 km/h
Fuel consumption: 6.3 l/100 km

Features: Full fairing.

Manufacturer: Kawasaki Heavy Industries Ltd.

KAWASAKI (Japan)

Model: ZXR750

Engine: 4-str LC dohc 4-valve
in-line four
Capacity: 749 cc
Bore × Stroke: 71 × 47.3 mm
Compression ratio: 10.8:1
Carburettor: 4 × 38 mm Keihin cv
Maximum power: 110 bhp at
10 500 rpm
Starting: electric

Transmission: 6-speed chain

Electrics: 12 v digital ignition
with 8 Ah battery

Frame: Diamond section
aluminium perimeter

Suspension: 43 mm upside
down telescopic fork with
adjustable 'Uni-Trak' system

Brakes: Twin 320 mm front
discs and rear 230 mm disc

Tyres: Front is 120/70VR17
Rear is 180/55VR17

Dimensions:
Length: 2 090 mm
Width: 755 mm
Wheelbase: 1 420 mm
Clearance: 145 mm
Seat height: 780 mm
Dry weight: 195 kg
Fuel tank: 18 litres

Performance:
Top speed: 250 km/h
Fuel consumption: 7 l/100 km

Features: Race replica styling.
The ZXR 750R is a superbike racer
version in limited production.

Manufacturer: Kawasaki Heavy Industries Ltd.

KAWASAKI (Japan)

Model: GPX750R

Engine: 4-str LC dohc 4-valve
in-line four
Capacity: 748 cc
Bore × Stroke: 68 × 51.5 mm
Compression ratio: 11.2:1
Carburettor: 4 × 34 mm Keihin cv
Maximum power: 88 bhp at
11 000 rpm
Starting: electric

Transmission: 6-speed chain

Electrics: 12 v electronic
ignition with 14 Ah battery

Frame: High tensile steel cradle

Suspension: Telescopic fork
with ESCS and rear air adjustable
Uni-Trak system

Brakes: Twin 242 mm discs and
rear 202 mm disc

Tyres: Front is 110/90V16
Rear is 140/70V18

Dimensions:
Length: 2 170 mm
Width: 715 mm
Wheelbase: 1 460 mm
Clearance: 150 mm
Seat height: 775 mm
Dry weight: 195 kg
Fuel tank: 21 litres

Performance:
Top speed: 235 km/h
Fuel consumption: 7 l/100 km

Features: Full fairing,
Electronic Suspension Control
System on front fork.

Manufacturer: Kawasaki Heavy Industries Ltd.

KAWASAKI (Japan)

Model: Tengai KL650

Engine: 4-str LC dohc 4-valve
single
Capacity: 651 cc
Bore × Stroke: 100 × 83 mm
Compression ratio: 9.5:1
Carburettor: 40 mm Keihin cv
Maximum power: 48 bhp at
6 500 rpm
Starting: electric

Transmission: 5-speed chain

Electrics: 12 v CDI ignition

Frame: Semi-double cradle

Suspension: Air-adjustable
front fork with rear *Uni-Trak*
system

Brakes: 252 mm front disc and
rear 204 mm disc

Tyres: Front is 90/90–21
Rear is 130/80–17

Dimensions:
Length: 2 220 mm
Width: 920 mm
Wheelbase: 1 480 mm
Clearance: 210 mm
Seat height: 870 mm
Dry weight: 159 kg
Fuel tank: 23 litres

Performance:
Top speed: 165 km/h
Fuel consumption: 5.5 l/100 km

Features: Desert Racer styling.
Enclosed front disc. Engine bash-
plate, hand guards, rear carrier.

Manufacturer: Kawasaki Heavy Industries Ltd.

KAWASAKI (Japan)

Model: ZZ-R600

Engine: 4-str LC dohc 4-valve
in-line four
Capacity: 599 cc
Bore × Stroke: 64 × 46.6 mm
Compression ratio: 11.5:1
Carburettor: 4 × 36 mm Keihin cv
Maximum power: 98 bhp at
11 500 rpm
Starting: electric

Transmission: 6-speed chain

Electrics: 12 v digital ignition
with 12 Ah battery

Frame: Aluminium box section
perimeter

Suspension: 41 mm telescopic
front fork with rear adjustable
Uni-Trak system

Brakes: Twin 300 mm front
discs and rear 230 mm disc

Tyres: Front is 120/60VR17
Rear is 160/60VR17

Dimensions:
Length: 2 075 mm
Width: 700 mm
Wheelbase: 1 440 mm
Clearance: 110 mm
Seat height: 780 mm
Dry weight: 195 kg
Fuel tank: 18 litres

Performance:
Top speed: 230 km/h
Fuel consumption: 6.8 l/100 km

Features: Full fairing with
lockable compartments.
Supersport class winner.

Manufacturer: Kawasaki Heavy Industries Ltd.

KAWASAKI (Japan)

Model: GPZ550

Engine: 4-str dohc in-line four
Capacity: 553 cc
Bore × Stroke: 58 × 52.4 mm
Compression ratio: 10:1
Carburettor: 4 × 27 mm Tekei
Maximum power: 65 bhp at
10 500 rpm
Starting: electric

Transmission: 6-speed chain

Electrics: 12 v electronic
ignition with 12 Ah battery

Frame: Tubular double cradle

Suspension: Air adjustable
front fork with anti-dive and rear
Uni-Trak system

Brakes: 226 mm triple disc
system

Tyres: Front is 100/90–18
Rear is 120/80–18

Dimensions:
Length: 2 205 mm
Width: 720 mm
Wheelbase: 1 445 mm
Clearance: 160 mm
Seat height: 780 mm
Dry weight: 191 kg
Fuel tank: 18 litres

Performance:
Top speed: 200 km/h
Fuel consumption: 6 l/100 km

Features: Handle-bar fairing.

Manufacturer: Kawasaki Heavy Industries Ltd.

KAWASAKI (Japan)

Model: Zephyr 550

Engine: 4-str dohc in-line four
Capacity: 553 cc
Bore × Stroke: 58 × 52.4 mm
Compression ratio: 9.5:1
Carburettor: 4 × 30 mm Keihin cv
Maximum power: 50 bhp at
10 000 rpm
Starting: electric

Transmission: 6-speed chain

Electrics: 12 v digital ignition
with 12 Ah battery

Frame: High-tensile steel cradle

Suspension: 39 mm telescopic
front fork with twin rear
piggyback gas shocks

Brakes: Twin 300 mm front
discs and rear 245 mm disc

Tyres: Front is 110/80–17
Rear is 140/70–18

Dimensions:
Length: 2 080 mm
Width: 755 mm
Wheelbase: 1 435 mm
Clearance: 120 mm
Seat height: 770 mm
Dry weight: 179 kg
Fuel tank: 15 litres

Performance:
Top speed: 190 km/h
Fuel consumption: 5 l/100 km

Features: Back-to-basics
model. 4-into-1 exhaust. Oil
cooler. Alloy wheels. Also a 750 cc
version.

Manufacturer: Kawasaki Heavy Industries Ltd

KAWASAKI (Japan)

Model: GPZ500S

Engine: 4-str LC dohc 4-valve
twin
Capacity: 498 cc
Bore × Stroke: 74 × 58 mm
Compression ratio: 10.8:1
Carburettor: 2 × 34 mm Keihin cv
Maximum power: 60 bhp at
9 800 rpm
Starting: electric

Transmission: 6-speed chain

Electrics: 12 v electronic
ignition with 14 Ah battery

Frame: Box section cradle

Suspension: Telehydraulic
front fork with rear adjustable
Uni-Trak system

Brakes: 252 mm front disc and
160 mm rear drum

Tyres: Front is 100/90H16
Rear is 120/90H16

Dimensions:
Length: 2 110 mm
Width: 675 mm
Wheelbase: 1 440 mm
Clearance: 120 mm
Seat height: 770 mm
Dry weight: 169 kg
Fuel tank: 18 litres

Performance:
Top speed: 205 km/h
Fuel consumption: 6.2 l/100 km

Features: Full fairing and belly
pan.

Manufacturer: Kawasaki Heavy Industries Ltd.

KAWASAKI (Japan)

Model: KLE500

Engine: 4-str LC dohc 4-valve twin
Capacity: 498 cc
Bore × Stroke: 74 × 58 mm
Compression ratio: 11:1
Carburettor: 2 × 34 mm Keihin
Maximum power: ...
Starting: electric

Transmission: 6-speed chain

Electrics: 12 v digital ignition with 8 Ah battery

Frame: Tubular double cradle

Suspension: 41 mm leading axle fork with 5-way adjustable rear *Uni-Trak* system

Brakes: 300 mm front disc and 230 mm rear disc

Tyres: Front is 90/90–21
Rear is 130/80–17

Dimensions:
Length: ...
Width: ...
Wheelbase: ...
Clearance: ...
Seat height: ...
Dry weight: ...
Fuel tank: 15 litres

Performance:
Top speed: ...
Fuel consumption: ...

Features: New dual-purpose machine. Fairing, engine bash-plate, rear carrier.

Manufacturer: Kawasaki Heavy Industries Ltd.

KAWASAKI (Japan)

Model: EN500

Engine: 4-str LC dohc 4-valve
twin
Capacity: 498 cc
Bore × Stroke: 74 × 58 mm
Compression ratio: 10.8:1
Carburettor: 2 × 34 mm Keihin cv
Maximum power: 50 bhp at
8 500 rpm
Starting: electric

Transmission: 6-speed belt
drive

Electrics: 12 v electronic
ignition with 12 Ah battery

Frame: Tubular double cradle

Suspension: 36 mm long
leading axle fork with twin
adjustable rear shocks

Brakes: 270 mm front disc and
180 mm rear drum

Tyres: Front is 100/90–19
Rear is 140/90–15

Dimensions:
Length: 2 265 mm
Width: 840 mm
Wheelbase: 1 555 mm
Clearance: 170 mm
Seat height: 730 mm
Dry weight: 186 kg
Fuel tank: 11 litres

Performance:
Top speed: 160 km/h
Fuel consumption: 5.5 l/100 km

Features: Custom styling.

Manufacturer: Kawasaki Heavy Industries Ltd.

KAWASAKI (Japan)

Model: ZXR400

Engine: 4-str LC dohc 4-valve
in-line four
Capacity: 398 cc
Bore × Stroke: 57 × 39 mm
Compression ratio: 12.1:1
Carburettor: 4 × 32 mm Keihin cv
Maximum power: 62 bhp at
12 500 rpm
Starting: electric

Transmission: 6-speed chain

Electrics: 12 v digital ignition
with 10 Ah battery

Frame: Aluminium diamond
section perimeter

Suspension: 41 mm upside
down front fork with rear
adjustable *Uni-Trak* system

Brakes: Twin 276 mm front
discs and 207 mm rear disc

Tyres: Front is 120/60VR17
Rear is 160/60VR17

Dimensions:
Length: 1 995 mm
Width: 700 mm
Wheelbase: 1 385 mm
Clearance: 120 mm
Seat height: 765 mm
Dry weight: 159 kg
Fuel tank: 16 litres

Performance:
Top speed: 225 km/h
Fuel consumption: 6 l/100 km

Features: Works-style chassis,
full fairing, push-to-cancel
indicators.

Manufacturer: Kawasaki Heavy Industries Ltd.

KAWASAKI (Japan)

Model: KR-1S

Engine: 2-str LC reed-valve
KIPS twin
Capacity: 249 cc
Bore × Stroke: 56 × 50.6 mm
Compression ratio: 7.4:1
Carburettor: 2 × 28 mm Keihin
Maximum power: 60 bhp at
9 500 rpm
Starting: kick

Transmission: 6-speed chain

Electrics: 12 v CDI ignition

Frame: Aluminium twin spar

Suspension: 41 mm telescopic
front fork with rear *Uni-Trak*
system

Brakes: Twin 247 mm front
discs and rear 187 mm disc

Tyres: Front is 100/70R17
Rear is 130/60R18

Dimensions:
Length: 2 005 mm
Width: 690 mm
Wheelbase: 1 365 mm
Clearance: 125 mm
Seat height: 750 mm
Dry weight: 123 kg
Fuel tank: 16 litres

Performance:
Top speed: 210 km/h
Fuel consumption: 7.4 l/100 km

Features: Super sports road
bike. Full fairing. Kawasaki
Integrated Power valve System.

Manufacturer: Kawasaki Heavy Industries Ltd.

KAWASAKI (Japan)

Model: ZZ-R250

Engine: 4-str LC dohc 4-valve twin
Capacity: 248 cc
Bore × Stroke: 62 × 41.2 mm
Compression ratio: 12.4:1
Carburettor: 2 × 30 mm Keihin cv
Maximum power: 35.5 bhp at 12 500 rpm
Starting: electric

Transmission: 6-speed chain

Electrics: 12 v electronic ignition with 8 Ah battery

Frame: Double box section aluminium diamond

Suspension: 37 mm telescopic front fork with rear *Uni-Trak* system

Brakes: 272 mm front disc and 193 mm rear disc

Tyres: Front is 100/80–17
Rear is 140/70–17

Dimensions:
Length: 2 050 mm
Width: 700 mm
Wheelbase: 1 405 mm
Clearance: 135 mm
Seat height: 760 mm
Dry weight: 148 kg
Fuel tank: 18 litres

Performance:
Top speed: 145 km/h
Fuel consumption: 4.6 l/100 km

Features: Full fairing with lockable compartment.

Manufacturer: Kawasaki Heavy Industries Ltd.

KAWASAKI (Japan)

Model: KMX200

Engine: 2-str LC reed-valve
single with KIPS
Capacity: 191 cc
Bore × Stroke: 67 × 54.4 mm
Compression ratio: 8:1
Carburettor: 26 mm Mikuni
Maximum power: 30 bhp at
8 500 rpm
Starting: kick

Transmission: 6-speed chain

Electrics: 12 v CDI ignition
with 4 Ah battery

Frame: Tubular semi-double
cradle

Suspension: Air adjustable
front tork with rear *Uni-Trak*
system

Brakes: 213 mm front disc and
183 mm rear disc

Tyres: Front is 3.00–21
Rear is 4.60–17

Dimensions:
Length: 2 095 mm
Width: 830 mm
Wheelbase: 1 180 mm
Clearance: 285 mm
Seat height: 860 mm
Dry weight: 100 kg
Fuel tank: 9.3 litres

Performance:
Top speed: 136 km/h
Fuel consumption: 6 l/100 km

Features: Moto-cross styled
trail machine. Rear carrier. Also in
125 cc version.

Manufacturer: Kawasaki Heavy Industries Ltd.

KAWASAKI (Japan)

Model: KDX125SR

Engine: 2-str LC reed-valve with KIPS single
Capacity: 124 cc
Bore × Stroke: 56 × 50.6 mm
Compression ratio: 8:1
Carburettor: 28 mm Keihin
Maximum power: 12 bhp at 8 000 rpm
Starting: kick

Transmission: 6-speed chain

Electrics: 12 v CDI ignition with 3 Ah battery

Frame: High tensile steel perimeter

Suspension: 41 mm telescopic front fork with rear *Uni-Trak* system

Brakes: 220 mm front disc and 190 mm rear disc

Tyres: Front is 70/100–21
Rear is 4.10–18

Dimensions:
Length: 2 120 mm
Width: 875 mm
Wheelbase: 1 400 mm
Clearance: 250 mm
Seat height: 860 mm
Dry weight: 107 kg
Fuel tank: 9 litres

Performance:
Top speed: 115 km/h
Fuel consumption: 5 l/100 km

Features: Hi-tech trail bike. Hand guards. Full power version available. Kawasaki Integrated Power-valve System (KIPS).

Manufacturer: Kawasaki Heavy Industries Ltd.

KAWASAKI (Japan)

Model: AR125

Engine: 2-str LC rotary and
reed-valve single
Capacity: 123 cc
Bore × Stroke: 55 × 51.8 mm
Compression ratio: 7:1
Carburettor: 26 mm Mikuni
Maximum power: 12 bhp at
8 500 rpm
Starting: kick

Transmission: 6-speed chain

Electrics: 12 v CDI ignition
with 5 Ah battery

Frame: Tubular double cradle

Suspension: Telescopic front
fork with rear *Uni-Trak* system

Brakes: 260 mm front disc and
rear 130 mm drum

Tyres: Front is 2.75–18
Rear is 3.00–18

Dimensions:
Length: 2 030 mm
Width: 675 mm
Wheelbase: 1 115 mm
Clearance: 170 mm
Seat height: 795 mm
Dry weight: 107 kg
Fuel tank: 11.5 litres

Performance:
Top speed: 120 km/h
Fuel consumption: 4.4 l/100 km

Features: Full fairing. Sports
learner bike. Full power version
available.

Manufacturer: Kawasaki Heavy Industries Ltd.

KAWASAKI (Japan)

Model: KH125

Engine: 2-str rotary disc-valve single
Capacity: 123 cc
Bore × Stroke: 55 × 51.8 mm
Compression ratio: 7.3:1
Carburettor: 22 mm Mikuni
Maximum power: 12 bhp at 8 000 rpm
Starting: kick

Transmission: 5-speed chain

Electrics: 12 v magneto ignition with 5 Ah battery

Frame: Tubular double cradle

Suspension: Telescopic front fork with twin 5-way adjustable rear shocks

Brakes: 210 mm front disc and 130 mm rear drum

Tyres: Front is 2.75–18
Rear is 3.00–18

Dimensions:
Length: 1 925 mm
Width: 745 mm
Wheelbase: 1 260 mm
Clearance: 150 mm
Seat height: 780 mm
Dry weight: 95.5 kg
Fuel tank: 13.5 litres

Performance:
Top speed: 115 km/h
Fuel consumption: 4.2 l/100 km

Features: Commuter bike.

Manufacturer: Kawasaki Heavy Industries Ltd.

KAWASAKI (Japan)

Model: AR50

Engine: 2-str reed-valve single
Capacity: 49 cc
Bore × Stroke: 39 × 41.6 mm
Compression ratio: 7:1
Carburettor: 14 mm Mikuni
Maximum power: 2.9 bhp at
4 500 rpm
Starting: kick

Transmission: 5-speed chain

Electrics: 6 v CDI ignition

Frame: Tubular, semi-double
cradle

Suspension: Telehydraulic
front fork with rear *Uni-Trak*
system

Brakes: 210 mm front disc and
110 mm rear drum

Tyres: Front is 2.50–18
Rear is 2.75–18

Dimensions:
Length: 1 880 mm
Width: 630 mm
Wheelbase: 1 195 mm
Clearance: 175 mm
Seat height: 785 mm
Dry weight: 78 kg
Fuel tank: 9.6 litres

Performance:
Top speed: 56 km/h
Fuel consumption: 4 l/100 km

Features: Sports moped. Range
also includes 6-speed 80 cc
version.

Manufacturer: Kawasaki Heavy Industries Ltd.

KTM (Austria)

Model: KTM 600 LC4

Engine: 4-str LC 4-valve single
Capacity: 553 cc
Bore × Stroke: 95 × 78 mm
Compression ratio: 9.5:1
Carburettor: 38 mm Dell'Orto
Maximum power: 52 bhp at
8 500 rpm
Starting: kick

Transmission: 5-speed chain

Electrics: 12 v electronic
ignition

Frame: Chrome-moly steel
cradle

Suspension: White Power
front fork with rear *Pro-Lever*
monoshock

Brakes: 240 mm front disc and
220 mm rear disc

Tyres: Front is 90/90–21
Rear is 140/80–18

Dimensions:
Length: 2 190 mm
Width: ...
Wheelbase: 1 510 mm
Clearance: 355 mm
Seat height: 955 mm
Dry weight: 128 kg
Fuel tank: 8.5 litres

Performance:
Top speed: ...
Fuel consumption: ...

Features: Stone protector on
front fork, anti-slide seat cover.

Manufacturer: KTM Motor-Fahrzeugbau AG., Postfach 66, A-5230
Mattighofen, Austria.

KTM (Austria)

Model: KTM 300 Enduro

Engine: 2-str LC reed-valve
single
Capacity: 297 cc
Bore × Stroke: 72 × 73 mm
Compression ratio: 15:1
Carburettor: 37 mm Keihin
Maximum power: 50 bhp at
7 500 rpm
Starting: kick

Transmission: 5-speed chain

Electrics: 12 v electronic
ignition

Frame: Chrome-moly cradle

Suspension: Upside down
White Power fork with rear *Pro
Link* monoshock

Brakes: 240 mm front disc and
220 mm rear disc

Tyres: Front is 90/90–21
Rear is 140/80–18

Dimensions:
Length: 2 160 mm
Width: ...
Wheelbase: 1 485 mm
Clearance: 385 mm
Seat height: 945 mm
Dry weight: 112 kg
Fuel tank: 9.8 litres

Performance:
Top speed: ...
Fuel consumption: ...

Features: Front fork stone
protector.

Manufacturer: KTM Motor Fahrzeugbau AG.

KTM (Austria)

Model: KTM 125 Enduro

Engine: 2-str LC reed-valve
single
Capacity: 124.8 cc
Bore × Stroke: 54.25 × 54 mm
Compression ratio: 14:1
Carburettor: 37 mm Dell'Orto
Maximum power: 36 bhp at
11 500 rpm
Starting: kick

Transmission: 6-speed chain

Electrics: 6 v Motoplat ignition

Frame: Chrome-moly cradle

Suspension: Upside-down
White Power fork with rear *Pro-
Link* monoshock

Brakes: 240 mm front disc and
220 mm rear disc

Tyres: Front is 90/90–21
Rear is 120/90–18

Dimensions:
Length: 2 090 mm
Width: ...
Wheelbase: 1 435 mm
Clearance: 380 mm
Seat height: 950 mm
Dry weight: 99 kg
Fuel tank: 9 litres

Performance:
Top speed: ...
Fuel consumption: ...

Features: Mint and Pepper side
covers and rear fender. Exhaust
silencer with sound-insulating
material.

Manufacturer: KTM Motor Fahrzeugbau AG.

LAVERDA (Italy)

Model: Navarro

Engine: 2-str LC single
Capacity: 124.63 cc
Bore × Stroke: 56 × 50.6 mm
Compression ratio: 12:1
Carburettor: 28 mm Dell'Orto
Maximum power: 22 bhp at
10 500 rpm
Starting: electric

Transmission: 7-speed chain

Electrics: 12 v electronic
ignition with 9 Ah battery

Frame: Steel trellis

Suspension: Marzocchi front
forks with rear *Soft-Ramble*
monoshock

Brakes: 298 mm single disc
240 mm rear disc

Tyres: Front is 100/80–16
Rear is 130/70–17

Dimensions:
Length: 2 030 mm
Width: 700 mm
Wheelbase: 1410 mm
Clearance: 170 mm
Seat height: 800 mm
Dry weight: 129 kg
Fuel tank: 14 litres

Performance:
Top speed: 160 km/h
Fuel consumption: 5 l/100 km

Features: Racing type bean can
exhaust.

Manufacturer: Nuova Moto Laverda, 36042 Breganze(VI), Italy.

LAVERDA (Italy)

Model: Toledo

Engine: 2-str LC single
Capacity: 123.63 cc
Bore × Stroke: 54 × 54 mm
Compression ratio: 14:1
Carburettor: 28 mm Dell'Orto
Maximum power: 17 bhp at
8 600 rpm
Starting: electric

Transmission: 5-speed chain

Electrics: 12 v electronic
ignition with 9 Ah battery

Frame: Steel trellis

Suspension: Marzocchi front
forks with twin rear hydraulic
shocks

Manufacturer: Nuova Moto Laverda.

Brakes: 298 mm drilled disc and
127 mm rear drum

Tyres: Front is 1.85–19
Rear is 2.50–16

Dimensions:
Length: 2 155 mm
Width: 800 mm
Wheelbase: 1470 mm
Clearance: 230 mm
Seat height: 800 mm
Dry weight: 127 kg
Fuel tank: 14 litres

Performance:
Top speed: 130 km/h
Fuel consumption: 5 l/100 km

Features: West Coast styling.

LAVERDA (Italy)

Model: Gaucho

Engine: 2-str LC single
Capacity: 49.9 cc
Bore × Stroke: 38 × 44 mm
Compression ratio: 11.5:1
Carburettor: 14–12 mm Dell'Orto
Maximum power: ...
Starting: electric

Transmission: 3-speed chain

Electrics: 12 v electronic
ignition with 4 Ah battery

Frame: Tubular single cradle

Suspension: Marzocchi front
fork with rear *Soft-Ramble*
monoshock

Brakes: 220 mm drilled disc
front and rear

Tyres: Front is 1.50–21
Rear is 1.85–18

Dimensions:
Length: 1 985 mm
Width: 850 mm
Wheelbase: 1350 mm
Clearance: 320 mm
Seat height: 850 mm
Dry weight: 95 kg
Fuel tank: 12 litres

Performance:
Top speed: 40 km/h
Fuel consumption: 2.5 l/100 km

Features:

Manufacturer: Nuova Moto Laverda.

MALAGUTI (Italy)

Model: RST 50

Engine: 2-str LC reed-valve
single
Capacity: 50 cc
Bore × Stroke: 30 × 41.8 mm
Compression ratio: 10:1
Carburettor: Dell'Orto
Maximum power: 1.5 bhp at
6 200 rpm
Starting: kick

Transmission: 3-speed chain

Electrics: 12 v electronic
ignition

Frame: Box section cradle

Suspension: Telehydraulic fork
with anti-dive and rear
monoshock

Brakes: 220 mm front disc and
200 mm rear disc

Tyres: Front is 2.75–16
Rear is 3.25–16

Dimensions:
Length: ...
Width: ...
Wheelbase: ...
Clearance: ...
Seat height: ...
Dry weight: 78 kg
Fuel tank: 9 litres

Performance:
Top speed: 40 km/h
Fuel consumption: 1.8 l/100 km

Features: Full enclosed
bodywork with twin headlights.

Manufacturer: Malaguti S.p.A., via Emilia Levante, 498, 40068 S.
Lazzaro di Savena (BO), Italy.

MALAGUTI (Italy)

Model: MRX 50

Engine: 2-str LC single
Capacity: 50 cc
Bore × Stroke: 30 × 41.8 mm
Compression ratio: 10:1
Carburettor: Dell'Orto
Maximum power: 1.5 bhp at
6 200 rpm
Starting: kick

Transmission: 3-speed chain

Electrics: 12 v electronic
ignition

Frame: Tubular cradle

Suspension: Telehydraulic
front fork with rear monoshock
system

Manufacturer: Malaguti S.p.A.

Brakes: Shrouded front disc
and rear 130 mm drum

Tyres: Front is 2.75–21
Rear is 3.50–18

Dimensions:
Length: ...
Width: ...
Wheelbase: ...
Clearance: ...
Seat height: ...
Dry weight: 78 kg
Fuel tank: 9 litres

Performance:
Top speed: 40 km/h
Fuel consumption: 2.3 l/100 km

Features: Self-lubrication
system, hand guards and rear
carrier.

MALAGUTI (Italy)

Model: Fifty Top 50

Engine: 2-str LC reed-valve single
Capacity: 49 cc
Bore × Stroke: 39 × 41.8 mm
Compression ratio: 10:1
Carburettor: Dell'Orto
Maximum power: 1.5 bhp at 3 800 rpm
Starting: kick

Transmission: 3-speed chain

Electrics: 12 v electronic ignition

Frame: Pressed steel step-thru

Suspension: Telehydraulic leading link fork with rear monoshock system

Manufacturer: Malaguti S.p.A.

Brakes: Enclosed front disc and rear drum

Tyres: Front is 2.75–16
Rear is 3.25–16

Dimensions:
Length: ...
Width: ...
Wheelbase: ...
Clearance: ...
Seat height: ...
Dry weight: 62 kg
Fuel tank: 3 litres

Performance:
Top speed: 40 km/h
Fuel consumption: 1.9 l/100 km

Features: Other models include the 50 Mistral and Fifty Full CX.

MBK (France)

Model: ZX50 Trail

Engine: 2-str single
Capacity: 49.9 cc
Bore × Stroke: 40 × 39.2 mm
Compression ratio: 11:1
Carburettor: 14 mm Dell'Orto
Maximum power: 4.8 bhp at
7 000 rpm
Starting: kick

Transmission: Automatic

Electrics: 12 v CDI ignition
with 3 Ah battery

Frame: Tubular cradle

Suspension: Long travel
telehydraulic fork with rear *Mono
Cross* system

Brakes: 110 mm drums front
and rear

Tyres: Front is 2.50–21
Rear is 3.25–18

Dimensions:
Length: 2 120 mm
Width: 800 mm
Wheelbase: 1 355 mm
Clearance: 208 mm
Seat height: 820 mm
Dry weight: 87 kg
Fuel tank: 11.5 litres

Performance:
Top speed: . . .
Fuel consumption: . . .

Features: Rear carrier. Engine
protector.

Manufacturer: MBK Industrie, Z.I. de Rouvroy, 02100 Saint-Quentin,
France.

MONTESA (Spain)

Model: Cota 335

Engine: 2-str single
Capacity: 327.8 cc
Bore × Stroke: 83.4 × 60 mm
Compression ratio: 9.5:1
Carburettor: 27 mm Amal
Maximum power: 17.5 bhp
Starting: kick

Transmission: 6-speed chain

Electrics: 6 v flywheel magneto
ignition

Frame: Duplex tubular cradle

Suspension: Telescopic front
fork with rear monoshock system

Brakes: 185 mm drilled disc and
175 mm rear disc

Tyres: Front is 2.75–21
Rear is 4.00–18

Dimensions:
Length: 2 010 mm
Width: 802 mm
Wheelbase: 1 320 mm
Clearance: 350 mm
Seat height: 805 mm
Dry weight: 89 kg
Fuel tank: 5 litres

Performance:
Top speed: ...
Fuel consumption: ...

Features: Most powerful of the
Montesa trial bikes.

Manufacturer: Montesa Honda SA., 08940 Cornella de Llobregat,
Barcelona, Spain.

MOTO GUZZI (Italy)

Model: 1000 Daytona i.e.

Engine: 4-str dohc 4-valve 90°
vee-twin
Capacity: 992 cc
Bore × Stroke: 90 × 78 mm
Compression ratio: 10:1
Carburettor: Injection
Maximum power: 92 bhp at
7 600 rpm
Starting: electric

Transmission: 5-speed shaft
drive

Electrics: 12 v digital ignition
with 12 Ah battery

Frame: Box section single beam

Suspension: Telehydraulic
front fork with rear *Koni*
monoshock

Brakes: Twin 300 mm Brembo
discs and rear 280 mm disc

Tyres: Front is 120/70ZR17
Rear is 160/60ZR18 tubeless

Dimensions:
Length: 2 160 mm
Width: 700 mm
Wheelbase: 1 520 mm
Clearance: 130 mm
Seat height: 750
Dry weight: 205 kg
Fuel tank: 25 litres

Performance:
Top speed: 245 km/h
Fuel consumption: 6.2 l/100 km

Features: Weber Marelli
electronic fuel injection.

Manufacturer: GBM S.p.A., via E.V. Parodi, 57, 22054 Mandello del
Lario (CO), Italy.

MOTO GUZZI (Italy)

Model: Le Mans 1000

Engine: 4-str ohv 90° vee-twin
Capacity: 948.8 cc
Bore × Stroke: 88 × 78 mm
Compression ratio: 10:1
Carburettor: 2 × 40 mm Dell'Orto
Maximum power: 82 bhp at
7 500 rpm
Starting: electric

Transmission: 5-speed shaft
drive

Electrics: 12 v coil ignition with
24 Ah battery

Frame: Duplex tubular cradle

Suspension: Telescopic air fork
with twin *Koni* rear shocks

Manufacturer: GBM S.p.A.

Brakes: 270 mm triple discs
with integral braking system

Tyres: Front is 100/90V18
Rear is 120/90V18

Dimensions:
Length: 2 160 mm
Width: 690 mm
Wheelbase: 1 514 mm
Clearance: 120 mm
Seat height: 750 mm
Dry weight: 215 kg
Fuel tank: 25 litres

Performance:
Top speed: 230 km/h
Fuel consumption: 5.4 l/100 km

Features: Front and back brake
operated by foot pedal, 1000S is a
similar model without the fairing
and bellypan.

MOTO GUZZI (Italy)

Model: SP1000 III Spada

Engine: 4-str ohv 4-valve 90°
vee-twin
Capacity: 948.8 cc
Bore × Stroke: 88 × 78 mm
Compression ratio: 9.5:1
Carburettor: 2 × 36 mm Dell'Orto
Maximum power: 71 bhp at
6 800 rpm
Starting: electric

Transmission: 5-speed shaft
drive

Electrics: 12 v electronic
ignition with 24 Ah battery

Frame: Duplex tubular cradle

Suspension: Telescopic air fork
with twin adjustable rear shocks

Manufacturer: GBM S.p.A.

Brakes: Twin 300 mm discs and
rear 270 mm disc

Tyres: Front is 110/90V18
Rear is 120/90V18

Dimensions:
Length: 2 180 mm
Width: 750 mm
Wheelbase: 1 480 mm
Clearance: 150 mm
Seat height: 750 mm
Dry weight: 230 kg
Fuel tank: 22.5 litres

Performance:
Top speed: 195 km/h
Fuel consumption: 5.6 l/100 km

Features: Integrated fairing
and large capacity panniers

MOTO GUZZI (Italy)

Model: Mille GT

Engine: 4-str ohv 4-valve 90°
vee-twin
Capacity: 949 cc
Bore × Stroke: 88 × 78 mm
Compression ratio: 9.2:1
Carburettor: 2 × 30 mm Dell'Orto
Maximum power: 67 bhp at
6 700 rpm
Starting: electric

Transmission: 5-speed shaft
drive

Electrics: 12 v electronic
ignition

Frame: Duplex tubular cradle

Suspension: Telescopic air fork
with twin *Koni* rear shocks

Manufacturer: GBM S.p.A.

Brakes: Twin 300 mm front
discs and rear 242 mm disc

Tyres: Front is 110/90–18
Rear is 120/90–18

Dimensions:
Length: 2 200 mm
Width: 760 mm
Wheelbase: 1 505 mm
Clearance: 150 mm
Seat height: 807 mm
Dry weight: 215 kg
Fuel tank: 24 litres

Performance:
Top speed: 200 km/h
Fuel consumption: 5.8 l/100 km

Features: The GT series
includes the Sessantacinque
(650 cc) and Trentacinque
(350 cc) versions.

MOTO GUZZI (Italy)

Model: 1000 California III

Engine: 4-str ohv 90° vee-twin
Capacity: 948.8 cc
Bore × Stroke: 88 × 78 mm
Compression ratio: 9.2:1
Carburettor: Injection
Maximum power: 67 bhp at
6 800 rpm
Starting: electric

Transmission: 5-speed shaft
drive

Electrics: 12 v digital ignition
with 12 Ah battery

Frame: Duplex tubular cradle

Suspension: *Bitubo* adjustable
telescopic fork with twin *Koni*
rear shocks

Manufacturer: GBM S.p.A.

Brakes: Twin 300 mm front
discs and 270 mm rear disc

Tyres: Front is 110/90V18
Rear is 130/80V18 tubeless

Dimensions:
Length: 2 260 mm
Width: ...
Wheelbase: 1 550 mm
Clearance: 160 mm
Seat height: 749 mm
Dry weight: 270 kg
Fuel tank: 25 litres

Performance:
Top speed: 190 km/h
Fuel consumption: 5.7 l/100 km

Features: Integral braking
system. Also in carburettor
version. Top box and panniers.

MOTO GUZZI (Italy)

Model: QUOTA 1000

Engine: 4-str ohv 90° vee-twin
Capacity: 948.8 cc
Bore × Stroke: 88 × 78 mm
Compression ratio: 10:1
Carburettor: Fuel injection
Maximum power: 75 bhp at
7 400 rpm
Starting: electric

Transmission: 5-speed shaft
drive

Electrics: 12 v digital ignition

Frame: Box section cradle

Suspension: Telehydraulic
front fork with *Marzocchi*
monoshock

Manufacturer: GBM S.p.A.

Brakes: 300 mm front disc and
280 mm rear disc

Tyres: Front is 90/90–21
Rear is 130/80–17

Dimensions:
Length: ...
Width: ...
Wheelbase: ...
Clearance: ...
Seat height: ...
Dry weight: 210 kg
Fuel tank: 22 litres

Performance:
Top speed: 192 km/h
Fuel consumption: 5.2 l/100 km

Features: Twin headlamp
fairing, rear carrier, hand guards.

MOTO GUZZI (Italy)

Model: Targa 750

Engine: 4-str ohv 90° vee-twin
Capacity: 743.9 cc
Bore × Stroke: 80 × 74 mm
Compression ratio: 9.7:1
Carburettor: 2 × 30 mm Dell'Orto
Maximum power: 48 bhp at
6 600 rpm
Starting: electric

Transmission: 5-speed shaft
drive

Electrics: 12 v electronic
ignition with 24 Ah battery

Frame: Duplex tubular cradle

Suspension: Telescopic front
fork with twin adjustable rear
shocks

Manufacturer: GBM S.p.A.

Brakes: Twin 270 mm front
discs and rear 235 mm disc

Tyres: Front is 100/90V18
Rear is 120/80V18

Dimensions:
Length: 2 160 mm
Width: 690 mm
Wheelbase: 1 514 mm
Clearance: 120 mm
Seat height: 750 mm
Dry weight: 180 kg
Fuel tank: 16.5 litres

Performance:
Top speed: 185 km/h
Fuel consumption: 5 l/100 km

Features: Styled like the Le
Mans

MOTO GUZZI (Italy)

Model: 750 Nevada

Engine: 4-str ohv 90° vee-twin
Capacity: 743.5 cc
Bore × Stroke: 80 × 74 mm
Compression ratio: 9.6:1
Carburettor: 2 × 30 mm Dell'Orto
Maximum power: 48 bhp at
6 600 rpm
Starting: electric

Transmission: 5-speed shaft
drive

Electrics: 12 v electronic
ignition with 20 Ah battery

Frame: Duplex tubular cradle

Suspension: Telehydraulic
front fork with twin *Bitubo* rear
shocks

Manufacturer: GBM S.p.A.

Brakes: Twin 270 mm front
discs and rear 260 mm disc

Tyres: Front is 100/90V18
Rear is 130/60V16

Dimensions:
Length: 2 260 mm
Width: ...
Wheelbase: 1 498 mm
Clearance: 190 mm
Seat height: 812 mm
Dry weight: 177 kg
Fuel tank: 16.5 litres

Performance:
Top speed: 165 km/h
Fuel consumption: 5.4 l/100 km

Features: Street cruiser styling.

MOTO GUZZI (Italy)

Model: NTX 650

Engine: 4-str ohv 90° vee-twin
Capacity: 643.4 cc
Bore × Stroke: 80 × 64 mm
Compression ratio: 10:1
Carburettor: 2 × 30 mm Dell'Orto
Maximum power: 48 bhp at
7 400 rpm
Starting: electric

Transmission: 5-speed shaft
drive

Electrics: 12 v electronic
ignition with 20 Ah battery

Frame: Tubular cradle

Suspension: *Marzocchi* front
fork with twin adjustable rear
shocks

Manufacturer: GBM S.p.A.

Brakes: 260 mm discs front and
rear

Tyres: Front is 3.00–21
Rear is 4.00–18

Dimensions:
Length: 2 250 mm
Width: 900 mm
Wheelbase: 1 480 mm
Clearance: 250 mm
Seat height: 840 mm
Dry weight: 170 kg
Fuel tank: 32 litres

Performance:
Top speed: 170 km/h
Fuel consumption: 5.5 l/100 km

Features: Carrier and engine
bashplate. Model range includes
NTX 750 and 350 versions.

MORINI (Italy)

Model: Dart 350

Engine: 4-str ohv 72° vee-twin
Capacity: 344 cc
Bore × Stroke: 62 × 57 mm
Compression ratio: 11:1
Carburettor: 2 × 25 mm Dell'Orto
Maximum power: 34 bhp at
8 500 rpm
Starting: electric

Transmission: 6-speed chain

Electrics: 12 v electronic
ignition with 18 Ah battery

Frame: Aluminium beam type

Suspension: Telehydraulic
front fork with rear *Morini
System* monoshock

Brakes: 300 mm front disc and
240 mm rear disc

Tyres: Front is 2.50–16
Rear is 3.00–17

Dimensions:
Length: 1 960 mm
Width: 625 mm
Wheelbase: 1 390 mm
Clearance: 170 mm
Seat height: 770 mm
Dry weight: 150 kg
Fuel tank: 14 litres

Performance:
Top speed: 170 km/h
Fuel consumption: 5 l/100 km

Features: Enclosed bodywork
and wrap-round front mudguard.

Manufacturer: Moto Morini S.p.A., via Bergami, 7, 40133 Bologna,
Italy.

MORINI (Italy)

Model: Excalibur

Engine: 4-str ohv 72° vee-twin
Capacity: 344 cc
Bore × Stroke: 62 × 57 mm
Compression ratio: 11:1
Carburettor: 2 × 25 mm Dell'Orto
Maximum power: 34 bhp at
7 800 rpm
Starting: electric and kick

Transmission: 6-speed chain

Electrics: 12 v electronic
ignition

Frame: Duplex tubular cradle

Suspension: Telehydraulic
front fork with twin adjustable
rear dampers

Manufacturer: Motor Morini S.p.A.

Brakes: 260 mm front disc and
240 mm rear disc

Tyres: Front is 100/90–18
Rear is 130/90–16

Dimensions:
Length: 2 200 mm
Width: 1 010 mm
Wheelbase: 1 515 mm
Clearance: 174 mm
Seat height: 750 mm
Dry weight: 168 kg
Fuel tank: 17 litres

Performance:
Top speed: 155 km/h
Fuel consumption: 5 l/100 km

Features: Custom-style with
rear backrest and carrier. Also in
42 bhp 507 cc version.

MZ (Germany)

Model: ETZ 301

Engine: 2-str single
Capacity: 291 cc
Bore × Stroke: 75.5 × 65 mm
Compression ratio: 10:1
Carburettor: 26 mm BVF
Maximum power: 23 bhp at
5 500 rpm
Starting: kick

Transmission: 5-speed chain

Electrics: 12 v coil ignition with
5.5 Ah battery

Frame: Welded box section
bridge

Suspension: Telescopic front
fork with twin adjustable rear
shocks

Brakes: 280 mm front disc and
160 mm rear drum

Tyres: Front is 90/90–18S
Rear is 110/80–16S

Dimensions:
Length: 2 005 mm
Width: 915 mm
Wheelbase: 1 340 mm
Clearance: 150 mm
Seat height: 775 mm
Dry weight: 128 kg
Fuel tank: 17 litres

Performance:
Top speed: 135 km/h
Fuel consumption: 5 l/100 km

Features: Cockpit fairing, fully-
enclosed chain. Also available as
243 cc version, the ETZ 251.

Manufacturer: MZ-Motorradwerk Zschopau GmbH, PSF 72,
Zschopau-9360, Germany.

MZ (Germany)

Model: ETZ 125

Engine: 2-str single
Capacity: 123 cc
Bore × Stroke: 52 × 58 mm
Compression ratio: 10.5:1
Carburettor: ...
Maximum power: 10.5 bhp at
6 000 rpm
Starting: kick

Transmission: 5-speed chain

Electrics: 12 v dynamo and coil
ignition with 5.5 Ah battery

Frame: Welded steel bridge
type

Suspension: Telescopic front
fork with twin adjustable rear
shocks

Brakes: 280 mm front disc and
rear 150 mm drum

Tyres: Front is 2.75–18
Rear is 3.25–16

Dimensions:
Length: 1 978 mm
Width: 915 mm
Wheelbase: 1 175 mm
Clearance: 150 mm
Seat height: 820 mm
Dry weight: 109 kg
Fuel tank: 13 litres

Performance:
Top speed: 100 km/h
Fuel consumption: 3 l/100 km

Features: Fully-enclosed chain.
Available in 150 version and in off-
road rig.

Manufacturer: MZ-Motorradwerk Zschopau GmbH.

NEVAL (USSR)

Model: Dnepr 16

Engine: 4-str ohv flat twin
Capacity: 649 cc
Bore × Stroke: 78 × 68 mm
Compression ratio: 8.5:1
Carburettor: 2 × K301
Maximum power: 36 bhp at 5 300 rpm
Starting: side kick

Transmission: 4-speed shaft drive with reverse

Electrics: 12 v coil ignition with 2 × 6 v batteries

Frame: Steel double cradle

Suspension: Telescopic front fork with twin adjustable rear shocks

Brakes: Drums front and rear

Tyres: 3.75–19 front and rear

Dimensions:
Length: 2 430 mm
Width: 1 700 mm
Wheelbase: 1 510 mm
Clearance: 125 mm
Seat height: 825 mm
Dry weight: 355 kg
Fuel tank: 18 litres

Performance:
Top speed: 120 km/h (sidecar)
Fuel consumption: 6 l/100 km

Features: Foot pedal gear shift. Military sidecar has twin wheel drive, brake and interchangeable spare wheel.

Manufacturer: Russian built and distributed by Neval Motorcycles Ltd., 'Brockholme', Seaton Road, Hornsea, England HU18 1BZ.

NEVAL (USSR)

Model: Soviet Knight

Engine: 4-str ohv flat twin
Capacity: 649 cc
Bore × Stroke: 78 × 68 mm
Compression ratio: 8.5:1
Carburettor: 2 × 28 mm K62
Maximum power: 36 bhp at
5 300 rpm
Starting: kick

Transmission: 4-speed shaft
drive

Electrics: 12 v electronic
ignition

Frame: Steel tubular cradle

Suspension: Telescopic front
fork with adjustable rear shocks

Brakes: Twin leading shoe
drums front and rear

Tyres: 3.75–19 front and rear

Dimensions:
Length: 2 430 mm
Width: 900 mm
Wheelbase: 1 500 mm
Clearance: 130 mm
Seat height: 825 mm
Dry weight: 210 kg
Fuel tank: 18 litres

Performance:
Top speed: 150 km/h
Fuel consumption: 6 l/100 km

Features: Single or dual saddle,
leather saddlebags, pull-back
bars, crash bars. Options include
fairings.

Manufacturer: Neval Motorcycles Ltd.

NORTON (United Kingdom)

Model: F1

Engine: Twin-chamber LC
rotary
Capacity: 588 cc
Bore × Stroke: n/a
Compression ratio: 9:1
Carburettor: 2 × 34 mm Mikuni
Maximum power: 95 bhp at
9 500 rpm
Starting: electric

Transmission: 5-speed chain

Electrics: 12 v electronic
ignition with 14 Ah battery

Frame: Twin spar aluminium
alloy beam

Suspension: *White Power*
upside down fork with rear *White
Power* monoshock

Brakes: Twin 320 mm floating
discs and 230 mm rear disc

Tyres: Front is 120/70ZR17
Rear is 170/60ZR17 tubeless

Dimensions:
Length: 2 060 mm
Width: 740 mm
Wheelbase: 1 440 mm
Clearance: 175 mm
Seat height: 760 mm
Dry weight: 192 kg
Fuel tank: 20 litres

Performance:
Top speed: 225 km/h
Fuel consumption: 8 l/100 km

Features: Race replica. JPS
version outputs 135 bhp.

Manufacturer: Norton Motors Ltd., Lynn Lane, Shenstone, Staffs
WS14 0EA, England.

NORTON (United Kingdom)

Model: Commander

Engine: Twin-chamber LC rotary
Capacity: 588 cc
Bore × Stroke: n/a
Compression ratio: 9:1
Carburettor: 2 × 38 SU cv
Maximum power: 85 bhp at 9 000 rpm
Starting: electric

Transmission: 5-speed chain

Electrics: 12 v electronic ignition

Frame: Pressed steel monocoque

Suspension: 37 mm telescopic fork with twin rear gas shocks

Brakes: Twin slotted 265 mm discs and rear 265 mm disc

Tyres: Front is 100/90V18 Rear is 110/90V18 tubeless

Dimensions:
Length: 2 200 mm
Width: 880 mm
Wheelbase: 1 486 mm
Clearance: 180 mm
Seat height: 830 mm
Dry weight: 235 kg
Fuel tank: 23 litres

Performance:
Top speed: 200 km/h
Fuel consumption: 6.2 l/100 km

Features: Daytime running lights. Twin panniers and full fairing. Also as police and paramedic machines. The Classic is unfaired version.

Manufacturer: Norton Motors Ltd.

PEUGEOT (France)

Model: XPS2 Avenger

Engine: 2-str single
Capacity: 49.1 cc
Bore × Stroke: 40 × 39.1 mm
Compression ratio: 8.5:1
Carburettor: 14 mm Dell'Orto
Maximum power: 4.8 bhp at
6 000 rpm
Starting: kick

Transmission: Automatic

Electrics: 12 v CDI ignition

Frame: Tubular double cradle

Suspension: Telescopic front
fork with rear *Mono Flex* system

Brakes: 118 mm drums front
and rear

Tyres: Front is 2.50–21
Rear is 3.00–18

Dimensions:
Length: 2 040 mm
Width: 810 mm
Wheelbase: 1 330 mm
Clearance: 250 mm
Seat height: 830 mm
Dry weight: 60 kg
Fuel tank: 9 litres

Performance:
Top speed: 80 km/h
Fuel consumption: 3 l/100 km

Features: Fairing and rear
carrier, engine protector and
aluminium silencer.

Manufacturer: Cycles Peugeot, 252 Boulevard Peraire, Paris, France.

PEUGEOT (France)

Model: STL2 Rapido

Engine: 2-str single
Capacity: 49.4 cc
Bore × Stroke: 41 × 37.4 mm
Compression ratio: 7:1
Carburettor: 12 mm Keihin
Maximum power: 3.6 bhp at
6 000 rpm
Starting: electric/kick

Transmission: automatic

Electrics: 12 v CDI ignition
with 4 Ah battery

Frame: Monocoque

Suspension: Telescopic front
fork with rear hydraulic
monoshock

Manufacturer: Cycles Peugeot

Brakes: 95 mm drums front and
rear

Tyres: 3.00–10 front and rear

Dimensions:
Length: 1 590 mm
Width: 650 mm
Wheelbase: 1 100 mm
Clearance: 135 mm
Seat height: 730 mm
Dry weight: 57 kg
Fuel tank: 5 litres

Performance:
Top speed: 50 km/h
Fuel consumption: 2.3 l/100 km

Features: Aluminium wheels,
sports-type exhaust. Front boot
and rear carrier.

PIAGGIO (Italy)

Model: Cosa 200

Engine: 2-str rotary-valve single
Capacity: 198 cc
Bore × Stroke: 66.6 × 57 mm
Compression ratio: 9.2:1
Carburettor: 24 mm Dell'Orto
Maximum power: 11 bhp at
6 000 rpm
Starting: electric

Transmission: 4-speed direct
drive

Electrics: 12 v electronic
ignition

Frame: Steel monocoque

Suspension: Single hydraulic
shocks front and rear with
variable dampening

Brakes: 170 mm linked drum
system

Tyres: 100/90–10 front and rear

Dimensions:
Length: 1 805 mm
Width: 700 mm
Wheelbase: 1 270 mm
Clearance: 200 mm
Seat height: 790 mm
Dry weight: 125 kg
Fuel tank: 7.8 litres

Performance:
Top speed: 99 km/h
Fuel consumption: 3 l/100 km

Features: Integral braking
system, elaborate
instrumentation, helmet fits
beneath the saddle. Also in
125/150 cc versions.

Manufacturer: Piaggio Veicoli Europei S.p.A., viale Rinaldo Piaggio,
23, 56025 Pontedera (PI), Italy.

PIAGGIO (Italy)

Model: PX 50XL Plurimatic

Engine: 2-str rotary valve single
Capacity: 49.28 cc
Bore × Stroke: 38.2 × 43 mm
Compression ratio: 9.25:1
Carburettor: Dell'Orto SHB 16/12
Maximum power: 2.3 bhp at
5 000 rpm
Starting: kick

Transmission: 3-speed belt
drive

Electrics: 6 v electronic ignition

Frame: Steel monocoque

Suspension: Variable pitch
helical spring with double action
shocks

Manufacturer: Piaggio V.E. S.p.A.

Brakes: 150 mm drums front
and rear

Tyres: 3.00–10 front and rear

Dimensions:
Length: 1 685 mm
Width: 700 mm
Wheelbase: 1 180 mm
Clearance: 200 mm
Seat height: 790 mm
Dry weight: 80 kg
Fuel tank: 6.4 litres

Performance:
Top speed: 40 km/h
Fuel consumption: 1.5 l/100 km

Features: Also available with
electric start.

SIMSON (Germany)

Model: S53 Comfort

Engine: 2-str single
Capacity: 49.8 cc
Bore × Stroke: 38 × 44 mm
Compression ratio: 9.5:1
Carburettor: 16 mm BVF
Maximum power: 4 bhp at
5 500 rpm
Starting: kick

Transmission: 4-speed chain

Electrics: 12 v electronic
ignition

Frame: Tubular bridge type

Suspension: Telescopic front
fork with twin hydraulic rear
shocks

Brakes: 125 mm drums front
and rear

Tyres: 2.75–16 front and rear

Dimensions:
Length: 1 890 mm
Width: 635 mm
Wheelbase: 1 210 mm
Clearance: 130 mm
Seat height: 760 mm
Dry weight: 78 kg
Fuel tank: 8 litres

Performance:
Top speed: 60 km/h
Fuel consumption: 2.5 l/100 km

Features: Cockpit fairing. Fully-
enclosed chain. Also as enduro
version.

Manufacturer: Simson Fahrzeug GmbH, PSF 140 Suhl 6000,
Germany.

SIMSON (Germany)

Model: SR50/1C Scooter

Engine: 2-str single
Capacity: 49.8 cc
Bore × Stroke: 38 × 44 mm
Compression ratio: 9.5:1
Carburettor: 16 mm BVF
Maximum power: 2.7 bhp at
5 500 rpm
Starting: kick

Transmission: 4-speed chain

Electrics: 12 v electronic
ignition with 5.5 Ah battery

Frame: Pressed steel
monocoque

Suspension: Long travel
telescopic fork, twin adjustable
rear shocks

Manufacturer: Simson Fahrzeug GmbH.

Brakes: 125 mm drums front
and rear

Tyres: 2.60–16 front and rear

Dimensions:
Length: 1 790 mm
Width: 874 mm
Wheelbase: 1 250 mm
Clearance: 130 mm
Seat height: 760 mm
Dry weight: 78 kg
Fuel tank: 6.5 litres

Performance:
Top speed: 60 km/h
Fuel consumption: 2.4 l/100 km

Features: Right side carrier.
Electric start version.

SUZUKI (Japan)

Model: VS1400GL Intruder

Engine: 4-str sohc 3-valve 45°
vee-twin
Capacity: 1 360 cc
Bore × Stroke: 94 × 98 mm
Compression ratio: 9.3:1
Carburettor: 2 × 36 mm Mikuni
Maximum power: 71 bhp at
4 800 rpm
Starting: electric

Transmission: 4-speed shaft
drive

Electrics: 12 v electronic
ignition with 14 Ah battery

Frame: Double tubular cradle

Suspension: Long travel
telehydraulic fork with twin
adjustable rear shocks

Brakes: 290 mm front disc and
275 mm rear disc

Tyres: Front is 110/90H19
Rear is 170/80H19

Dimensions:
Length: 2 230 mm
Width: 770 mm
Wheelbase: 1 620 mm
Clearance: 145 mm
Seat height: 720 mm
Dry weight: 243 kg
Fuel tank: 13 litres

Performance:
Top speed: 185 km/h
Fuel consumption: 6.6 l/100 km

Features: Harley-Davidson
lookalike. Air/oil cooling.

Manufacturer: Suzuki Motor Co. Ltd, 300 Takatsuka, Hamamatsu,
Japan.

SUZUKI (Japan)

Model: GSX1100F

Engine: 4-str SACS dohc
4-valve TSCC in-line four
Capacity: 1 127 cc
Bore × Stroke: 78 × 59 mm
Compression ratio: 10:1
Carburettor: 4 × 34 mm Mikuni
Maximum power: 125 bhp at
9 500 rpm
Starting: electric

Transmission: 5-speed chain

Electrics: 12 v digital ignition
with 14 Ah battery

Frame: Steel braced cradle

Suspension: Adjustable
telescopic fork with adjustable
Full Floater system

Brakes: 275 mm triple floating
disc system

Tyres: Front is 120/80VB16
Rear is 150/80VB16

Dimensions:
Length: 2 205 mm
Width: 765 mm
Wheelbase: 1 535 mm
Clearance: 130 mm
Seat height: 795 mm
Dry weight: 252 kg
Fuel tank: 21 litres

Performance:
Top speed: 250 km/h
Fuel consumption: 6 l/100 km

Features: Suzuki Advanced
Cooling System using oil. Twin
Swirl Combustion Chamber. 4-
into-2 exhaust, unique Power
Shield windscreen.

Manufacturer: Suzuki Motor Co. Ltd.

SUZUKI (Japan)

Model: GSX-R1100

Engine: 4-str SACS dohc
4-valve TSCC in-line four
Capacity: 1 127 cc
Bore × Stroke: 78 × 59 mm
Compression ratio: 10:1
Carburettor: 4 × 40 mm Mikuni
Maximum power: 143 bhp at
9 500 rpm
Starting: electric

Transmission: 5-speed chain

Electrics: 12 v electronic
ignition with 14 Ah battery

Frame: Race-style aluminium
cradle

Suspension: Upside down
adjustable fork with progressive
link system

Manufacturer: Suzuki Motor Co. Ltd.

Brakes: 310 mm twin floating
discs and 240 mm rear disc

Tyres: Front is 120/70ZR17
Rear is 180/55ZR17

Dimensions:
Length: 2 090 mm
Width: 755 mm
Wheelbase: 1 465 mm
Clearance: 120 mm
Seat height: 795 mm
Dry weight: 226 kg
Fuel tank: 22 litres

Performance:
Top speed: 270 km/h
Fuel consumption: 7.4 l/100 km

Features: Factory-racer styling
and technology. Full fairing with
cool air induction. Remote
reservoir rear shock.

SUZUKI (Japan)

Model: GSX1100G

Engine: 4-str SACS dohc
4-valve TSCC in-line four
Capacity: 1 127 cc
Bore × Stroke: 78 × 59 mm
Compression ratio: 10:1
Carburettor: 4 × 36 mm Mikuni
Maximum power: 125 bhp at
9 500 rpm
Starting: electric

Transmission: 5-speed shaft
drive

Electrics: 12 v digital ignition
with 12 Ah battery

Frame: Rigid double cradle

Suspension: 43 mm long travel
fork with progressive link rear
system

Manufacturer: Suzuki Motor Co. Ltd.

Brakes: Triple 275 mm floating
disc system

Tyres: Front is 110/80V18
Rear is 160/70V17

Dimensions:
Length: 2 220 mm
Width: 805 mm
Wheelbase: 1 568 mm
Clearance: 150 mm
Seat height: 805 mm
Dry weight: 240 kg
Fuel tank: 22 litres

Performance:
Top speed: 245 km/h
Fuel consumption: 6 l/100 km

Features: Traditional styling.
4-into-2 exhaust. Slingshot carbs.
Optional fairing and panniers.

SUZUKI (Japan)

Model: VX800

Engine: 4-str LC sohc 4-valve
TSCC vee-twin
Capacity: 805 cc
Bore × Stroke: 83 × 74.4 mm
Compression ratio: 10:1
Carburettor: 2 × 36 mm Mikuni
Maximum power: 63 bhp at
6 500 rpm
Starting: electric

Transmission: 5-speed shaft
drive

Electrics: 12 v digital ignition
with 16 Ah battery

Frame: Slim tubular cradle

Suspension: 41 mm long travel
fork with adjustable rear
piggyback shocks

Brakes: 310 mm front disc and
250 mm rear disc

Tyres: Front is 110/80–18
Rear is 150/70–17

Dimensions:
Length: 2 255 mm
Width: 805 mm
Wheelbase: 1 555 mm
Clearance: 145 mm
Seat height: 795 mm
Dry weight: 213 kg
Fuel tank: 19 litres

Performance:
Top speed: 190 km/h
Fuel consumption: 7 l/100 km

Features: Traditional-styled
sporting roadster. Reverse taper
exhausts.

Manufacturer: Suzuki Motor Co. Ltd.

SUZUKI (Japan)

Model: DR800S

Engine: 4-str SACS sohc
4-valve TSCC single
Capacity: 779 cc
Bore × Stroke: 105 × 90 mm
Compression ratio: 9.5:1
Carburettor: dual 33 mm Mikuni
Maximum power: 52.5 bhp at
7 000 rpm
Starting: electric

Transmission: 5-speed shaft
drive

Electrics: 12 v electronic
ignition with 14 Ah battery

Frame: Steel double cradle

Suspension: 41 mm long travel
fork with rear *Full Floater*
monoshock

Brakes: 280 mm front disc and
250 mm rear disc

Tyres: Front is 90/90–21
Rear is 130/80–17

Dimensions:
Length: 2 255 mm
Width: 945 mm
Wheelbase: 1 510 mm
Clearance: 235 mm
Seat height: 876 mm
Dry weight: 185 kg
Fuel tank: 29 litres

Performance:
Top speed: 180 km/h
Fuel consumption: 6 l/100 km

Features: Based on factory
Desert racer, DR-Zeta. Skid plate
and hand guards. Shrouded front
disc and fork.

Manufacturer: Suzuki Motor Co. Ltd.

SUZUKI (Japan)

Model: GSX-R750

Engine: 4-str SACS dohc TSCC
4-valve in-line four
Capacity: 749 cc
Bore × Stroke: 70 × 48.7 mm
Compression ratio: 10.9:1
Carburettor: 4 × 38 mm Mikuni
Maximum power: 120 bhp at
11 000 rpm
Starting: electric

Transmission: 6-speed chain

Electrics: 12 v electronic
ignition with 14 Ah battery

Frame: Box section aluminium
cradle

Suspension: Upside down
adjustable fork with progressive
link rear system

Brakes: Twin 310 mm floating
discs and rear 240 mm disc

Tyres: Front is 120/70ZR17
Rear is 170/60ZR17

Dimensions:
Length: 2 065 mm
Width: 725 mm
Wheelbase: 1 415 mm
Clearance: 125 mm
Seat height: 790 mm
Dry weight: 208 kg
Fuel tank: 21 litres

Performance:
Top speed: 256 km/h
Fuel consumption: 7 l/100 km

Features: Many racer-derived
lightweight features. Full fairing,
flush twin headlights. Slingshot
carbs. Remote reservoir rear
shock.

Manufacturer: Suzuki Motor Co. Ltd.

SUZUKI (Japan)

Model: GSX750F

Engine: 4-str SACS dohc
4-valve TSCC in-line four
Capacity: 748 cc
Bore × Stroke: 73 × 44.7 mm
Compression ratio: 10.7:1
Carburettor: 4 × 36 mm Mikuni
Maximum power: 106 bhp at
10 500 rpm
Starting: electric

Transmission: 6-speed chain

Electrics: 12 v electronic
ignition with 14 Ah battery

Frame: Box section double
cradle

Suspension: 41 mm adjustable
telescopic fork with rear *Full
Floater* system

Brakes: 290 mm twin floating
discs and 250 mm rear disc

Tyres: Front is 110/80V17
Rear is 150/70V17

Dimensions:
Length: 2 130 mm
Width: 730 mm
Wheelbase: 1 470 mm
Clearance: 140 mm
Seat height: 790 mm
Dry weight: 209 kg
Fuel tank: 20 litres

Performance:
Top speed: 230 km/h
Fuel consumption: 6.2 l/100 km

Features: Aerodynamic fairing
with Direct Air Intake System.
Slingshot carbs.

Manufacturer: Suzuki Motor Co. Ltd.

SUZUKI (Japan)

Model: VS750GLP

Engine: 4-str LC sohc 4-valve
TSCC 45° vee-twin
Capacity: 747 cc
Bore × Stroke: 80 × 74.4 mm
Compression ratio: 10:1
Carburettor: 2 × 34 mm Mikuni
Maximum power: 55 bhp at
7 500 rpm
Starting: electric

Transmission: 5-speed shaft
drive

Electrics: 12 v electronic
ignition with 14 Ah battery

Frame: Steel double cradle

Suspension: Long travel
telescopic fork with twin
adjustable rear shocks

Brakes: 310 mm front disc and
240 mm rear drum

Tyres: Front is 80/90–21
Rear is 140/90–15

Dimensions:
Length: 2 235 mm
Width: 750 mm
Wheelbase: 1 560 mm
Clearance: 135 mm
Seat height: 685 mm
Dry weight: 199 kg
Fuel tank: 12 litres

Performance:
Top speed: 170 km/h
Fuel consumption: 5.5 l/100 km

Features: Custom styling, tear
drop tank and pull-back bars. This
Intruder series includes a VS1400
model.

Manufacturer: Suzuki Motor Co. Ltd.

SUZUKI (Japan)

Model: DR650RSE

Engine: 4-str SACS dohc
4-valve Dual Plug single
Capacity: 641 cc
Bore × Stroke: 95 × 90.4 mm
Compression ratio: 9.7:1
Carburettor: 40 mm Mikuni
Maximum power: 46 bhp at
6 800 rpm
Starting: kick

Transmission: 5-speed chain

Electrics: 12 v electronic
ignition

Frame: Tubular cradle

Suspension: Long travel
telescopic fork with adjustable
Full Floater system

Brakes: 280 mm front disc and
250 mm rear disc

Tyres: Front is 90/90–21
Rear is 120/90–17

Dimensions:
Length: 2 235 mm
Width: 870 mm
Wheelbase: 1 510 mm
Clearance: 260 mm
Seat height: 890 mm
Dry weight: 155 kg
Fuel tank: 20 litres

Performance:
Top speed: 173 km/h
Fuel consumption: 5.2 l/100 km

Features: Half fairing. Skid
plate and rear carrier. Slingshot
carbs.

Manufacturer: Suzuki Motor Co. Ltd.

SUZUKI (Japan)

Model: GSX600F

Engine: 4-str SACS dohc
4-valve TSCC in-line four
Capacity: 599 cc
Bore × Stroke: 62.6 × 48.7 mm
Compression ratio: 11.3:1
Carburettor: 4 × 33 mm Mikuni
Maximum power: 86 bhp at
11 000 rpm
Starting: electric

Transmission: 6-speed chain

Electrics: 12 v electronic
ignition with 12 Ah battery

Frame: Box section double
cradle

Suspension: 41 mm telescopic
fork with adjustable *Full Floater*
monoshock

Brakes: 290 mm twin discs and
rear 250 mm disc

Tyres: Front is 140/80V17
Rear is 140/80V17

Dimensions:
Length: 2 110 mm
Width: 700 mm
Wheelbase: 1 430 mm
Clearance: 140 mm
Seat height: 780 mm
Dry weight: 210 kg
Fuel tank: 20 litres

Performance:
Top speed: 220 km/h
Fuel consumption: 6.3 l/100 km

Features: All-enclosed
bodywork. Derived from
GSX-R750.

Manufacturer: Suzuki Motor Co. Ltd.

SUZUKI (Japan)

Model: GS500E

Engine: 4-str dohc 4-valve
parallel twin
Capacity: 487 cc
Bore × Stroke: 74 × 56.6 mm
Compression ratio: 9:1
Carburettor: 2 × 33 mm Mikuni
Maximum power: 52 bhp at
9 200 rpm
Starting: electric

Transmission: 6-speed chain

Electrics: 12 v electronic
ignition with 8 Ah battery

Frame: Box section beam cradle

Suspension: Oil dampened
telescopic fork with rear
adjustable *Full Floater*

Manufacturer: Suzuki Motor Co. Ltd.

Brakes: 310 mm floating disc
and 250 mm rear disc

Tyres: Front is 110/80H17
Rear is 130/80H17

Dimensions:
Length: 2 075 mm
Width: 730 mm
Wheelbase: 1 405 mm
Clearance: 155 mm
Seat height: 785 mm
Dry weight: 169 kg
Fuel tank: 17 litres

Performance:
Top speed: 160 km/h
Fuel consumption: 6.4 l/100 km

Features: 2-into-1 exhaust.
Slingshot carbs.

SUZUKI (Japan)

Model: GSF400

Engine: 4-str LC dohc 4-valve
TSCC in-line four
Capacity: 398 cc
Bore × Stroke: 56 × 40.4 mm
Compression ratio: 11.8:1
Carburettor: 4 × 33 mm Mikuni
Maximum power: 54 bhp at
10 600 rpm
Starting: electric

Transmission: 6-speed chain

Electrics: 12 v electronic
ignition with 8 Ah battery

Frame: Steel tube diamond

Suspension: 41 mm telescopic
front fork with rear progressive
link system

Manufacturer: Suzuki Motor Co. Ltd.

Brakes: 310 mm front disc and
250 mm rear disc

Tyres: Front is 110/70–17
Rear is 150/70–17

Dimensions:
Length: 2 090 mm
Width: 730 mm
Wheelbase: 1 430 mm
Clearance: 155 mm
Seat height: 790 mm
Dry weight: 165 kg
Fuel tank: 16 litres

Performance:
Top speed: ...
Fuel consumption: ...

Features: Open styling. 4-into-1
exhaust, three-spoke wheels and
Slingshot carbs.

SUZUKI (Japan)

Model: DR350S

Engine: 4-str SACS sohc
4-valve single
Capacity: 349 cc
Bore × Stroke: 79 × 71.2 mm
Compression ratio: 9.5:1
Carburettor: 33 mm Mikuni
Maximum power: 23.5 bhp at
7 000 rpm
Starting: kick

Transmission: 6-speed chain

Electrics: 12 v electronic
ignition

Frame: Tubular cradle

Suspension: 43 mm adjustable
fork with remote reservoir *Showa*
rear shock

Manufacturer: Suzuki Motor Co. Ltd.

Brakes: 250 mm front disc and
220 mm rear disc

Tyres: Front is 80/100–21
Rear is 110/90–18

Dimensions:
Length: 2 090 mm
Width: 830 mm
Wheelbase: 1 435 mm
Clearance: 290 mm
Seat height: 919 mm
Dry weight: 118 kg
Fuel tank: 9 litres

Performance:
Top speed: ...
Fuel consumption: 6 l/100 km

Features: Dual purpose trail
bike. Skid plate and handlebar
protectors.

SUZUKI (Japan)

Model: RGV250

Engine: 2-str LC reed-valve
AETC 90° vee-twin
Capacity: 249 cc
Bore × Stroke: 56 × 50.6 mm
Compression ratio: 7.3:1
Carburettor: 2 × 34 mm Mikuni
Maximum power: 62 bhp at
11 000 rpm
Starting: kick

Transmission: 6-speed chain

Electrics: 12 v digital ignition
with 5 Ah battery

Frame: Box section aluminium
cradle

Suspension: Upside down
telescopic fork with adjustable
Full Floater system

Brakes: 300 mm twin floating
discs and 210 mm rear disc

Tyres: Front is 110/70R17
Rear is 150/60R17

Dimensions:
Length: 1 980 mm
Width: 690 mm
Wheelbase: 1 380 mm
Clearance: 125 mm
Seat height: 766 mm
Dry weight: 139 kg
Fuel tank: 16 litres

Performance:
Top speed: 210 km/h
Fuel consumption: 5.5 l/100 km

Features: Race-derived. Suzuki
Advanced Power Control engine
management. Automatic Exhaust
Timing Control. Dual right side
exhaust.

Manufacturer: Suzuki Motor Co. Ltd.

SUZUKI (Japan)

Model: GN250F

Engine: 4-str sohc 4-valve
single
Capacity: 249 cc
Bore × Stroke: 72 × 61.2 mm
Compression ratio: 8.9:1
Carburettor: 34 mm Mikuni
Maximum power: 22 bhp at
8 500 rpm
Starting: electric

Transmission: 5-speed chain

Electrics: 12 v electronic
ignition with 12 Ah battery

Frame: Tubular steel cradle

Suspension: Telescopic front
fork with twin adjustable rear
shocks

Manufacturer: Suzuki Motor Co. Ltd.

Brakes: Front disc and rear
drum

Tyres: Front is 3.00–18
Rear is 4.60–16

Dimensions:
Length: 2 035 mm
Width: 835 mm
Wheelbase: 1 350 mm
Clearance: 150 mm
Seat height: 680 mm
Dry weight: 129 kg
Fuel tank: 10.3 litres

Performance:
Top speed: 125 km/h
Fuel consumption: 4 l/100 km

Features: Custom styled. The
range also includes the LS650P
Savage.

SUZUKI (Japan)

Model: RG125

Engine: 2-str LC reed-valve
SAEC single
Capacity: 123 cc
Bore × Stroke: 54 × 54 mm
Compression ratio: 7.4:1
Carburettor: 28 mm Mikuni
Maximum power: 25 bhp at
8 500 rpm
Starting: kick

Transmission: 6-speed chain

Electrics: 12 v electronic
ignition with 4 Ah battery

Frame: Steel box section

Suspension: Telescopic front
fork with *Full Floater* monoshock

Brakes: Front disc and rear
drum

Tyres: Front is 80/90–16
Rear is 90/90–18

Dimensions:
Length: 2 030 mm
Width: 655 mm
Wheelbase: 1 310 mm
Clearance: 165 mm
Seat height: 730 mm
Dry weight: 106 kg
Fuel tank: 13 litres

Performance:
Top speed: 136 km/h
Fuel consumption: 4 l/100 km

Features: Suzuki Automatic
Exhaust Control. Frame mounted
fairing. Power restricted in France
and UK.

Manufacturer: Suzuki Motor Co. Ltd.

SUZUKI (Japan)

Model: GS125ES

Engine: 4-str sohc single
Capacity: 124 cc
Bore × Stroke: 57 × 48.8 mm
Compression ratio: 9.5:1
Carburettor: 24 mm Mikuni
Maximum power: 12 bhp at
9 500 rpm
Starting: electric

Transmission: 5-speed chain

Electrics: 12 v electronic
ignition

Frame: Tubular single cradle

Suspension: Telescopic front
fork with twin adjustable rear
shocks

Brakes: Front disc and rear
drum

Tyres: Front is 2.75–18
Rear is 3.00–18

Dimensions:
Length: 1 945 mm
Width: 710 mm
Wheelbase: 1 270 mm
Clearance: 170 mm
Seat height: 745 mm
Dry weight: 103 kg
Fuel tank: 11 litres

Performance:
Top speed: 116 km/h
Fuel consumption: 3 l/100 km

Features: Twin Dome
Combustion Chamber. Quarter
fairing.

Manufacturer: Suzuki Motor Co. Ltd.

SUZUKI (Japan)

Model: TS125R

Engine: 2-str LC piston and
reed-valve single
Capacity: 124.6 cc
Bore × Stroke: 56 × 50.6 mm
Compression ratio: 7.3:1
Carburettor: 24 mm Mikuni
Maximum power: 12 bhp at
9 800 rpm
Starting: kick

Transmission: 6-speed chain

Electrics: 12 v digital CD
ignition with 4 Ah battery

Frame: Tubular cradle

Suspension: Long travel
telescopic fork with rear
adjustable *Full Floater*

Brakes: 220 mm disc front and
rear

Tyres: Front is 2.75–21
Rear is 4.10–18

Dimensions:
Length: 2 170 mm
Width: 830 mm
Wheelbase: 1 415 mm
Clearance: 290 mm
Seat height: 900 mm
Dry weight: 109 kg
Fuel tank: 9.5 litres

Performance:
Top speed: 110 km/h
Fuel consumption: 4.2 l/100 km

Features: Styled on Suzuki RM
moto cross bikes. Unrestricted
versions, capable of 135 km/h.

Manufacturer: Suzuki Motor Co. Ltd.

SUZUKI (Japan)

Model: AE50 Style

Engine: 2-str single
Capacity: 49 cc
Bore × Stroke: 41 × 37.8 mm
Compression ratio: 7.1:1
Carburettor: 14 mm Mikuni
Maximum power: 2.9 bhp at
6 500 rpm
Starting: electric/kick

Transmission: V-belt
automatic

Electrics: 12 v electronic
ignition with 5 Ah battery

Frame: Monocoque

Suspension: Telescopic front
fork with oil dampened rear
swinging arm

Manufacturer: Suzuki Motor Co. Ltd.

Brakes: Drum front and rear

Tyres: 2.75–10 front and rear

Dimensions:
Length: 1 700 mm
Width: 660 mm
Wheelbase: 1 135 mm
Clearance: 100 mm
Seat height: 610 mm
Dry weight: 59 kg
Fuel tank: 4 litres

Performance:
Top speed: 56 km/h
Fuel consumption: 2 l/100 km

Features: Automatic choke.
Push-cancel indicators. Rear
carrier and storage compartment.
CP80 is larger engine version.

TRIUMPH (United Kingdom)

Model: Trophy 1200

Engine: 4-str LC dohc 4-valve
in-line four
Capacity: 1 180 cc
Bore × Stroke: 76 × 65 mm
Compression ratio: 10.6:1
Carburettor: 4 × 36 mm Mikuni
cv
Maximum power: 125 bhp at
9 000 rpm
Starting: electric

Transmission: 6-speed chain

Electrics: 12 v digital ignition
with 14 Ah battery

Frame: High tensile steel
tubular spine

Suspension: 43 mm telescopic
fork with rear gas-charged
monoshock

Brakes: Twin 296 mm floating
discs and 255 mm rear disc

Tyres: Front is 120/70V17
Rear is 160/60V18

Dimensions:
Length: 2 160 mm
Width: 740 mm
Wheelbase: 1 490 mm
Clearance: 160 mm
Seat height: 800 mm
Dry weight: 240 kg
Fuel tank: 25 litres

Performance:
Top speed: 240 km/h
Fuel consumption: 7.2 l/100 km

Features: Fully-enclosed
fairing. Sports-tourer model.

Manufacturer: Triumph Motorcycles Ltd, Jacknell Road, Hinckley,
Leics., LE10 3BS, United Kingdom.

TRIUMPH (United Kingdom)

Model: Daytona 1000

Engine: 4-str LC dohc 4-valve in-line four
Capacity: 998 cc
Bore × Stroke: 76 × 55 mm
Compression ratio: 11:1
Carburettor: 4 × 36 mm Mikuni cv
Maximum power: 121 bhp at 10 500 rpm
Starting: electric

Transmission: 6-speed chain

Electrics: 12 v digital ignition with 14 Ah battery

Frame: High tensile steel spine

Suspension: 43 mm adjustable telescopic fork with rear gas-charged monoshock

Brakes: Twin 310 mm floating discs and 255 mm rear disc

Tyres: Front is 130/60V17
Rear is 170/60V18

Dimensions:
Length: 2 160 mm
Width: 740 mm
Wheelbase: 1 490 mm
Clearance: 160 mm
Seat height: 780 mm
Dry weight: 235 kg
Fuel tank: 25 litres

Performance:
Top speed: ...
Fuel consumption: ...

Features: Twin headlight fairing, sports exhaust and white-faced instruments.

Manufacturer: Triumph Motorcycles Ltd.

TRIUMPH (United Kingdom)

Model: Trident 750

Engine: 4-str LC dohc 4-valve
in-line triple
Capacity: 749 cc
Bore × Stroke: 76 × 55 mm
Compression ratio: 11:1
Carburettor: 3 × 36 mm Mikuni
cv
Maximum power: 90 bhp at
10 500 rpm
Starting: electric

Transmission: 6-speed chain

Electrics: 12 v digital ignition

Frame: High tensile steel spine

Suspension: 43 mm adjustable
telescopic fork with rear gas-
charged monoshock

Brakes: Twin 296 mm floating
discs and rear 255 mm disc

Tyres: Front is 120/70V17
Rear is 160/60V18

Dimensions:
Length: 2 160 mm
Width: 740 mm
Wheelbase: 1 490 mm
Clearance: 160 mm
Seat height: 800 mm
Dry weight: 212 kg
Fuel tank: 25 litres

Performance:
Top speed: ...
Fuel consumption: ...

Features: Also in 900 version
developing 100 bhp.

Manufacturer: Triumph Motorcycles Ltd.

YAMAHA (Japan)

Model: VMX1200 V-MAX

Engine: 4-str LC dohc 4-valve
vee four
Capacity: 1 198 cc
Bore × Stroke: 76 × 66 mm
Compression ratio: 10.5:1
Carburettor: 4 × 35 mm Mikuni
Maximum power: 95.2 bhp at
8 000 rpm
Starting: electric

Transmission: 5-speed shaft
drive

Electrics: 12 v electronic
ignition

Frame: Double cradle

Suspension: Long travel
telescopic fork with adjustable
rear shocks

Brakes: 282 mm triple disc
system

Tyres: Front is 110/90V18
Rear is 150/90V15

Dimensions:
Length: 2 300 mm
Width: 795 mm
Wheelbase: 1 590 mm
Clearance: 145 mm
Seat height: 765 mm
Dry weight: 262 kg
Fuel tank: 15 litres

Performance:
Top speed: 218 km/h
Fuel consumption: . . .

Features: Richly chromed
muscle bike in 'Hot Rod' style.
Polished dished alloy wheels.
Distinctive air scoops.

Manufacturer: Yamaha Motor Co. Ltd, Shizuoka-ken, PO Box 1,
Iwata, Japan.

YAMAHA (Japan)

Model: FJ1200

Engine: 4-str dohc 4-valve
parallel four
Capacity: 1 188 cc
Bore × Stroke: 77 × 63.8 mm
Compression ratio: 9.7:1
Carburettor: 4 × 36 mm Mikuni
Maximum power: 125 bhp at
9 000 rpm
Starting: electric

Transmission: 5-speed chain

Electrics: 12 v electronic
ignition with 14 Ah battery

Frame: Perimeter lateral

Suspension: Telescopic front
fork with anti-dive and rear
Monocross

Brakes: 282 mm triple disc
system

Tyres: Front is 120/70V17
Rear is 150/80V16

Dimensions:
Length: 2 230 mm
Width: 775 mm
Wheelbase: 1 490 mm
Clearance: 140 mm
Seat height: 780 mm
Dry weight: 238 kg
Fuel tank: 22 litres

Performance:
Top speed: 240 km/h
Fuel consumption: 7 l/100 km

Features: Standard and high
windshields available. First
Japanese production bike with
anti-lock brakes.

Manufacturer: Yamaha Motor Co. Ltd.

YAMAHA (Japan)

Model: XV1100

Engine: 4-str sohc vee-twin
Capacity: 1 063 cc
Bore × Stroke: 95 × 75 mm
Compression ratio: 8.3:1
Carburettor: 2 × 40 mm Mikuni
Maximum power: 61 bhp at
6 000 rpm
Starting: electric

Transmission: 5-speed shaft
drive

Electrics: 12 v electronic
ignition with 14 Ah battery

Frame: Monocoque beam
chassis

Suspension: Telescopic front
fork with twin 4-way adjustable
rear shocks

Manufacturer: Yamaha Motor Co. Ltd.

Brakes: Twin 267 mm discs and
200 mm rear drum

Tyres: Front is 100/90-19H
Rear is 140/90-15H

Dimensions:
Length: 2 285 mm
Width: 840 mm
Wheelbase: 1 525 mm
Clearance: 145 mm
Seat height: 715 mm
Dry weight: 221 kg
Fuel tank: 16.8 litres

Performance:
Top speed: 185 km/h
Fuel consumption: 5 l/100 km

Features: Cruiser styling with
chromed exhausts, back rest and
hand-painted fuel tank.

YAMAHA (Japan)

Model: FZR1000

Engine: 4-str LC dohc 5-valve
parallel four
Capacity: 1 002 cc
Bore × Stroke: 75.5 × 56 mm
Compression ratio: 12:1
Carburettor: 4 × 38 mm Mikuni
cv
Maximum power: 125 bhp at
10 000 rpm
Starting: electric

Transmission: 5-speed chain

Electrics: 12 v digital ignition
with 12 Ah battery

Frame: Aluminium Deltabox

Suspension: Upside down
front fork with *Monocross* rear
using gas/oil shocks

Manufacturer: Yamaha Motor Co. Ltd.

Brakes: Twin floating 320 mm
discs and 267 mm rear disc

Tyres: Front is 130/60VR17
Rear is 170/60VR17

Dimensions:
Length: 2 205 mm
Width: 745 mm
Wheelbase: 1 470 mm
Clearance: 135 mm
Seat height: 775 mm
Dry weight: 214 kg
Fuel tank: 19 litres

Performance:
Top speed: 260 km/h
Fuel consumption: 8.6 l/100 km

Features: EXUP power-valve
exhaust, 4-into-1 stainless steel
pipes, slant-nosed upper cowling,
redesigned switchgear.

YAMAHA (Japan)

Model: XJ900F

Engine: 4-str dohc parallel four
Capacity: 891 cc
Bore × Stroke: 68.5 × 60.5 mm
Compression ratio: 9.6:1
Carburettor: 4 × 36 mm Mikuni
Maximum power: 98 bhp at
9 000 rpm
Starting: electric

Transmission: 5-speed shaft
drive

Electrics: 12 v electronic
ignition with 14 Ah battery

Frame: Duplex tubular cradle

Suspension: Telescopic front
fork with twin adjustable rear
shocks

Manufacturer: Yamaha Motor Co. Ltd.

Brakes: 267 mm slotted disc
system

Tyres: Front is 100/90V18
Rear is 120/90V18

Dimensions:
Length: 2 235 mm
Width: 755 mm
Wheelbase: 1 490 mm
Clearance: 145 mm
Seat height: 780 mm
Dry weight: 218 kg
Fuel tank: 22 litres

Performance:
Top speed: 220 km/h.
Fuel consumption: 6.6 l/100 km

Features: Head fairing and
engine undercowl, oil cooler.

YAMAHA (Japan)

Model: TDM850

Engine: 4-str LC dohc 5-valve
parallel four
Capacity: 849 cc
Bore × Stroke: 89.5 × 67.5 mm
Compression ratio: 9.2:1
Carburettor: 2 × 38 mm Mikuni
Maximum power: 77 bhp at
7 500 rpm
Starting: electric

Transmission: 5-speed chain

Electrics: 12 v electronic
ignition with 10 Ah battery

Frame: Steel Delta-box

Suspension: Long travel
telescopic front fork with rear
adjustable *Monocross*

Manufacturer: Yamaha Motor Co. Ltd.

Brakes: 298 mm twin discs with
rear 245 mm disc

Tyres: Front is 110/80-18H
Rear is 150/70-17H

Dimensions:
Length: 2 225 mm
Width: 780 mm
Wheelbase: 1 475 mm
Clearance: 160 mm
Seat height: 795 mm
Dry weight: 199 kg
Fuel tank: 18 litres

Performance:
Top speed: 220 km/h
Fuel consumption: 6.6 l/100 km

Features: 1990 new direction
model. Fairing with dual halogen
lights.

YAMAHA (Japan)

Model: FZR750R (OW01)

Engine: 4-str LC dohc 5-valve parallel four
Capacity: 749 cc
Bore × Stroke: 72 × 46 mm
Compression ratio: 11.2:1
Carburettor: 4 × 38 mm Mikuni
Maximum power: 121 bhp at 12 000 rpm
Starting: electric

Transmission: 6-speed chain

Electrics: 12 v digital ignition with 10 Ah battery

Frame: Aluminium Deltabox

Suspension: Telescopic front fork with Ohlins race-type rear shock

Brakes: 320 mm twin disc and 267 mm single disc

Tyres: Front is 130/60ZR17
Rear is 180/55ZR17

Dimensions:
Length: 2 180 mm
Width: 705 mm
Wheelbase: 1 445 mm
Clearance: 120 mm
Seat height: 780 mm
Dry weight: 187 kg
Fuel tank: 19 litres

Performance:
Top speed: 240 km/h
Fuel consumption: 7 l/100 km

Features: Grand Prix design, EXUP exhaust power-valve, twin fresh air intakes. Twin headlights.

Manufacturer: Yamaha Motor Co. Ltd.

YAMAHA (Japan)

Model: XTZ750 Super Ténéré

Engine: 4-str LC dohc 5-valve parallel twin
Capacity: 749 cc
Bore × Stroke: 87 × 63 mm
Compression ratio: 9.5:1
Carburettor: 2 × 38 mm Mikuni
Maximum power: 70 bhp at 7 500 rpm
Starting: electric

Transmission: 5-speed chain

Electrics: 12 v digital ignition with 14 Ah battery

Frame: Duplex tubular cradle

Suspension: Telescopic front fork with rear *Monocross* system

Brakes: 245 mm triple disc system

Tyres: Front is 90/90-21 H
Rear is 140/80-17 H

Dimensions:
Length: 2 285 mm
Width: 815 mm
Wheelbase: 1 505 mm
Clearance: 240 mm
Seat height: 865 mm
Dry weight: 195 kg
Fuel tank: 26 litres

Performance:
Top speed: 185 km/h
Fuel consumption: 5.6 l/100 km

Features: Half fairing, Paris-Dakar styling, hand shields and bash plate, twin headlights.

Manufacturer: Yamaha Motor Co. Ltd.

YAMAHA (Japan)

Model: XTZ660 Ténéré

Engine: 4-str LC sohc 5-valve single
Capacity: 659 cc
Bore × Stroke: 95 × 84 mm
Compression ratio: 8.5:1
Carburettor: 26/35 Teikei
Maximum power: 48 bhp at 6 250 rpm
Starting: electric

Transmission: 5-speed chain

Electrics: 12 v CDI ignition with 5 Ah battery

Frame: High-tensile steel diamond type

Suspension: 43 mm long travel fork with rear adjustable Bilstein-type shock

Brakes: 282 mm shrouded front disc and 220 mm rear disc

Tyres: Front is 90/90–21
Rear is 120/90–17

Dimensions:
Length: 2 275 mm
Width: 850 mm
Wheelbase: 1 490 mm
Clearance: 245 mm
Seat height: 865 mm
Dry weight: 168 kg
Fuel tank: 20 litres

Performance:
Top speed: 165 km/h
Fuel consumption: 7 l/100 km

Features: Slimline bodywork, skid plate and rear carrier. Twin-choke YDIS carburettor. Oil tank in frame. Replaces XT600Z model.

Manufacturer: Yamaha Motor Co. Ltd

YAMAHA (Japan)

Model: FZR600

Engine: 4-str LC dohc 4-valve
parallel four
Capacity: 599 cc
Bore × Stroke: 59 × 54.8 mm
Compression ratio: 12:1
Carburettor: 4 × 32 mm Mikuni
Maximum power: 90 bhp at
10 500 rpm
Starting: electric

Transmission: 6-speed chain

Electrics: 12 v digital ignition
with 12 Ah battery

Frame: Genesis Deltabox

Suspension: Telescopic front
fork with rear *Monocross* system

Brakes: 298 mm twin discs and
245 mm rear disc

Tyres: Front is 110/70VR17
Rear is 140/60VR18

Dimensions:
Length: 2 170 mm
Width: 700 mm
Wheelbase: 1 425 mm
Clearance: 135 mm
Seat height: 785 mm
Dry weight: 181 kg
Fuel tank: 18 litres

Performance:
Top speed: 235 km/h
Fuel consumption: 6.4 l/100 km

Features: Full fairing, 4-into-1
tuned exhaust, twin headlights.

Manufacturer: Yamaha Motor Co. Ltd.

YAMAHA (Japan)

Model: XJ600

Engine: 4-str dohc parallel four
Capacity: 598 cc
Bore × Stroke: 58.5 × 55.7 mm
Compression ratio: 10.2:1
Carburettor: 4 × 30 mm Mikuni
Maximum power: 72 bhp at
10 000 rpm
Starting: electric

Transmission: 6-speed chain

Electrics: 12 v digital ignition
with 12 Ah battery

Frame: Duplex tubular cradle

Suspension: Telescopic front
fork with rear *Monocross* system

Brakes: 267 mm triple slotted
disc system

Tyres: Front is 90/90-18 H
Rear is 110/90-18 H

Dimensions:
Length: 2 145 mm
Width: 745 mm
Wheelbase: 1 430 mm
Clearance: 135 mm
Seat height: 790 mm
Dry weight: 188 kg
Fuel tank: 19 litres

Performance:
Top speed: 205 km/h
Fuel consumption: 6 l/100 km

Features: Streamlined head
fairing and engine undercowl.
Traditional sports tourer.

Manufacturer: Yamaha Motor Co. Ltd.

YAMAHA (Japan)

Model: XT600E

Engine: 4-str sohc 4-valve single
Capacity: 595 cc
Bore × Stroke: 95 × 84 mm
Compression ratio: 8.5 : 1
Carburettor: 26 mm Teikei
Maximum power: 45 bhp at 6 500 rpm
Starting: electric

Transmission: 5-speed chain

Electrics: 12 v CDI ignition with 5 Ah battery

Frame: Tubular diamond cradle

Suspension: Telescopic front fork with rear *Monocross* system

Brakes: 267 mm front disc and 220 mm rear disc

Tyres: Front is 90/90–21
Rear is 120/90–17

Dimensions:
Length: 2 210 mm
Width: 820 mm
Wheelbase: 1 445 mm
Clearance: 265 mm
Seat height: 885 mm
Dry weight: 155 kg
Fuel tank: 13 litres

Performance:
Top speed: 170 km/h
Fuel consumption: 5.8 l/100 km

Features: Head cowl with flush-mount headlight, oil tank in the frame. Range includes XT350 trail model.

Manufacturer: Yamaha Motor Co. Ltd.

YAMAHA (Japan)

Model: FZR400 RR SP

Engine: 4-str LC dohc 4-valve parallel four
Capacity: 399 cc
Bore × Stroke: 56 × 40.5 mm
Compression ratio: 12:1
Carburettor: 4 × 34 mm Mikuni
Maximum power: 59 bhp at 12 000 rpm
Starting: electric

Transmission: 6-speed chain

Electrics: 12 v Digital ignition with 12 Ah battery

Frame: Aluminium Deltabox

Suspension: Damping adjustable front fork with rear *Monocross* system

Manufacturer: Yamaha Motor Co. Ltd.

Brakes: 298 mm twin discs and 245 mm rear disc

Tyres: Front is 120/60R17
Rear is 160/60R17

Dimensions:
Length: 1 975 mm
Width: 705 mm
Wheelbase: 1 365 mm
Clearance: 125 mm
Seat height: 780 mm
Dry weight: 165 kg
Fuel tank: 15 litres

Performance:
Top speed: 220 km/h
Fuel consumption: 7 l/100 km

Features: EXUP power valve, 4-into-1 exhaust system, full fairing. Supplied with a personalised owner's pack.

YAMAHA (Japan)

Model: RD350LCF

Engine: 2-str LC Torque
induction parallel twin
Capacity: 347 cc
Bore × Stroke: 64 × 54 mm
Compression ratio: 6:1
Carburettor: 2 × 26 mm Mikuni
Maximum power: 63 bhp at
9 000 rpm
Starting: kick

Transmission: 6-speed chain

Electrics: 12 v CDI ignition
with 5 Ah battery

Frame: Tubular wide cradle

Suspension: Air-assisted
telescopic fork with rear
Monocross system

Brakes: 267 mm slotted triple
disc system

Tyres: Front is 90/90–18 H
Rear is 110/80–18 H

Dimensions:
Length: 2 095 mm
Width: 700 mm
Wheelbase: 1 385 mm
Clearance: 165 mm
Seat height: 790 mm
Dry weight: 141 kg
Fuel tank: 17 litres

Performance:
Top speed: 195 km/h
Fuel consumption: 7 l/100 km

Features: Power valve fitted,
bean type silencers.

Manufacturer: Yamaha Motor Co. Ltd.

YAMAHA (Japan)

Model: TZR250

Engine: 2-str LC reed-valve parallel twin with YPVS
Capacity: 249 cc
Bore × Stroke: 56.4 × 50 mm
Compression ratio: 5.9:1
Carburettor: 2 × 28 mm Mikuni
Maximum power: 50 bhp at 10 000 rpm
Starting: kick

Transmission: 6-speed chain

Electrics: 12 v CDI ignition with 5 Ah battery

Frame: Aluminium Deltabox

Suspension: Air-assisted telescopic fork with rear *Monocross* system

Brakes: 320 mm drilled disc and 210 mm rear disc

Tyres: Front is 100/80–17 H
Rear is 120/80–17 H

Dimensions:
Length: 2 055 mm
Width: 660 mm
Wheelbase: 1 375 mm
Clearance: 135 mm
Seat height: 760 mm
Dry weight: 128 kg
Fuel tank: 16 litres

Performance:
Top speed: 190 km/h
Fuel consumption: 7 l/100 km

Features: Yamaha Power Valve System, full fairing, race design.

Manufacturer: Yamaha Motor Co. Ltd.

YAMAHA (Japan)

Model: TDR

Engine: 2-str LC reed-valve
parallel twin
Capacity: 249 cc
Bore × Stroke: 56.4 × 50 mm
Compression ratio: 5.9:1
Carburettor: 2 × 28 mm Mikuni
Maximum power: 50 bhp
at 10 000 rpm
Starting: kick

Transmission: 6-speed chain

Electrics: 12 v CDI ignition

Frame: Duplex tubular cradle

Suspension: Telescopic front
fork with rear *Monocross* system

Brakes: 320 mm front disc and
210 mm rear disc

Tyres: Front is 100/90-18 H
Rear is 120/80-17 H

Dimensions:
Length: 2 080 mm
Width: 785 mm
Wheelbase: 1 385 mm
Clearance: 230 mm
Seat height: 820 mm
Dry weight: 137 kg
Fuel tank: 14 litres

Performance:
Top speed: 176 km/h
Fuel consumption: 6.4 l/100 km

Features: Yamaha Power-Valve
System, tank-mounted fairing.

Manufacturer: Yamaha Motor Co. Ltd.

YAMAHA (Japan)

Model: TZR125

Engine: 2-str LC reed-valve
single with YEIS
Capacity: 124 cc
Bore × Stroke: 56.4 × 50 mm
Compression ratio: 5.9:1
Carburettor: 26 mm Mikuni
Maximum power: 12 bhp at
7 500 rpm
Starting: kick

Transmission: 6-speed chain

Electrics: 12 v CDI ignition
with 5 Ah battery

Frame: Steel-pressed Deltabox

Suspension: Telescopic front
fork with rear *Monocross* system

Brakes: Slotted 245 mm disc
front and rear

Tyres: Front is 90/80–17
Rear is 100/90–18

Dimensions:
Length: 2 025 mm
Width: 695 mm
Wheelbase: 1 340 mm
Clearance: 135 mm
Seat height: 760 mm
Dry weight: 105 kg
Fuel tank: 12 litres

Performance:
Top speed: 115 km/h
Fuel consumption: 5.8 l/100 km

Features: Race replica for
learners, cast alloy wheels.
Yamaha Energy Induction System
boosts pulling power and helps
economy.

Manufacturer: Yamaha Motor Co. Ltd.

YAMAHA (Japan)

Model: DT125R

Engine: 2-str LC reed-valve single
Capacity: 124 cc
Bore × Stroke: 56 × 50.6 mm
Compression ratio: 6.8:1
Carburettor: 26 mm Mikuni
Maximum power: 12 bhp at 7 000 rpm
Starting: kick

Transmission: 6-speed chain

Electrics: 12 v CDI ignition with 5 Ah battery

Frame: Steel tubular cradle

Suspension: Telescopic front fork with rear *Monocross* system

Brakes: 220 mm disc front and rear with plastic guard

Tyres: Front is 2.75–21
Rear is 4.10–18

Dimensions:
Length: 2 160 mm
Width: 830 mm
Wheelbase: 1 415 mm
Clearance: 285 mm
Seat height: 845 mm
Dry weight: 109 kg
Fuel tank: 10 litres

Performance:
Top speed: 105 km/h
Fuel consumption: 5 l/100 km

Features: Sporting trail bike in motocross style. YEIS and Autolube oil injection system. Range also includes DT50MX.

Manufacturer: Yamaha Motor Co. Ltd.

YAMAHA (Japan)

Model: YB100

Engine: 2-str disc-valve single
Capacity: 97 cc
Bore × Stroke: 52 × 45.6 mm
Compression ratio: 6.5:1
Carburettor: 20 mm Mikuni
Maximum power: 9.8 bhp at
8 000 rpm
Starting: kick

Transmission: 4-speed
enclosed chain

Electrics: 6 v flywheel magneto
ignition

Frame: Pressed steel spine

Suspension: Telescopic front
fork with twin hydraulic rear
shocks

Manufacturer: Yamaha Motor Co. Ltd.

Brakes: 110 mm drums front
and rear

Tyres: 2.50–18 front and rear

Dimensions:
Length: 1 850 mm
Width: 735 mm
Wheelbase: 1 180 mm
Clearance: 140 mm
Seat height: 785 mm
Dry weight: 84 kg
Fuel tank: 8.6 litres

Performance:
Top speed: 104 km/h
Fuel consumption: 3.2 l/100 km

Features: Commuter roadster,
Autolube oil injection system.
Sealed drum brakes.

YAMAHA (Japan)

Model: CG50 JOG

Engine: 2-str reed-valve single
Capacity: 49 cc
Bore × Stroke: 40 × 39.2 mm
Compression ratio: 6.7:1
Carburettor: 12 mm Teikei
Maximum power: 3.9 bhp at
6 500 rpm
Starting: electric/kick

Transmission: V-belt
automatic drive

Electrics: 12 v CDI ignition

Frame: Monocoque

Suspension: Telescopic front
fork with rear monoshock system

Brakes: Drums front and rear

Tyres: 3.00–10 front and rear

Dimensions:
Length: 1 610 mm
Width: 625 mm
Wheelbase: 1 115 mm
Clearance: 95 mm
Seat height: 700 mm
Dry weight: 58 kg
Fuel tank: 3.5 litres

Performance:
Top speed: 48 km/h
Fuel consumption: 2 l/100 km

Features: Rear rack, lockable
helmet compartment.